Alexander Sutherland

The Kingdom of God and Problems of To-Day

Lectures Delivered before the Biblical Department of Vanderbilt University

Alexander Sutherland

The Kingdom of God and Problems of To-Day
Lectures Delivered before the Biblical Department of Vanderbilt University

ISBN/EAN: 9783337170134

Printed in Europe, USA, Canada, Australia, Japan

Cover: Foto ©Lupo / pixelio.de

More available books at **www.hansebooks.com**

THE KINGDOM OF GOD

AND PROBLEMS OF TO-DAY.

LECTURES
DELIVERED BEFORE THE BIBLICAL DEPARTMENT OF
VANDERBILT UNIVERSITY.

BY ALEXANDER SUTHERLAND, D.D.,
Toronto, Canada.

TORONTO:
WILLIAM BRIGGS.

MONTREAL:
C. W. COATES.

HALIFAX:
S. F. HUESTIS.

COPYRIGHTED, 1898,
BY BARBEE & SMITH, AGENTS.

CONTENTS.

	PAGE
GENERAL PRELUDE	vii

LECTURE I.
THE KINGDOM OF GOD IN CONCEPTION AND OUTLINE 1

LECTURE II.
THE PRINCIPLES AND POLITY OF THE KINGDOM OF GOD 35

LECTURE III.
TWO IMPORTANT ISSUES, AND HOW TO MEET THEM 81

LECTURE IV.
THE PROBLEM OF POVERTY 125

LECTURE V.
LABOR DISPUTES, AND HOW TO END THEM ... 165

LECTURE VI.
THE STABILITY, PERPETUITY, AND FINAL CONSUMMATION OF THE KINGDOM OF GOD ... 201

GENERAL PRELUDE.

"Dreamer of dreams, born out of my due time,
  Why should I strive to set the crooked straight?
Let it suffice me that my murmuring rime
  Beats with light wings against the ivory gate,
  Telling a tale not too importunate
To those who in the sleepy region stay,
Lulled by the singer of an empty day."

(Rev. William Bayard Hale, "The New Obedience," p. 84.)

"The prophet that hath a dream, let him tell a dream; and he that hath my word, let him speak my word faithfully." (Jer. xxiii. 28.)

GENERAL PRELUDE.

In discoursing upon a subject so large as the problems of modern society, and the relation of the kingdom of God thereto, it will be seen how impossible it is to cover the ground in the compass of half a dozen lectures. Almost every topic would require a volume—some of them more than one—for its complete elucidation. Whole sections will have to be omitted, and others touched upon very slightly. All that can be done at this time is to outline the nature, principles, and polity of that kingdom which, as I believe, it has been and still is God's purpose to establish in this world, and to show, by suggestion rather than by exhaustive treatment, that if men could be persuaded to accept those principles as a rule of life, and to adopt that polity as the basis of their social relations, all the problems which now disturb society would be quickly and easily solved.

It is not uncommon to find the themes which come within the domain of sociology treated in an abstruse way, and burdened with technical terms intelligible only to scholars; while to ordinary people the Babel (let me not say babble) of high-sounding words is as "the crackling of thorns under a pot." But if in this department of investigation there are truths which all men ought to know (and how can they be of practical value otherwise?), they must be expressed in terms intelligible to average men and women. Sociology, although the word has a formidable sound, is not an abstruse science. Its truths, while touching very complex conditions, are simple in themselves; and if in these lectures I avoid as much as possible the terminology of the schools, and utter my thoughts in the everyday language of the common people, the result, though disappointing to pedantic scholarship, may be all the more useful to the multitude, whose ideas regarding social duties, obligations, and relationships need to be clarified and turned into better channels.

If there is one subject upon which, at the present time, more than upon any other, ample data, clear thinking, and accurate statement are required, it is the complex science of sociology. And yet, outside of a limited number of volumes, there are few subjects upon which we have less of either. The reason is plain. A great many persons who do not take the trouble to ascertain the facts, and have never been trained to think clearly, have made their minds receptacles for a mass of crude, undigested notions which they dignify with the name of social science, and then pour them forth upon a long-suffering world as a panacea for all the social ills to which flesh is heir. And so it has come to pass that what is called socialism has been sadly misunderstood and misinterpreted alike by its friends and foes. Even when clearly apprehended, secular democratic socialism may not commend itself to thoughtful men; but it is important that we should understand just what it is before we either laud it as the highest wisdom, or denounce it as false and misleading.

And yet the wide discussion of social and sociological topics, even when the discussion proceeds, as it sometimes does, in ignorance of the facts, much more of the underlying principles, will result in good. If it does no more, it will call the attention of earnest Christian thinkers to those conditions of society which, in the opinion of men who are not mere alarmists, forebode disaster; and when once it is seen that we can not proceed safely on the ostrich-like plan of thrusting our heads into the sand and refusing to see or hear, it is likely that some remedy for real social ills will be sought with an earnestness that will itself presage success. In medical science diagnosis must precede prescription, unless we are content to go upon the old empirical plan of mixing sundry nostrums in hope that some one of them *may* hit the disease; and the same thing may hold true with respect to the diseases of the body politic.

It would be a great mistake to suppose that the social ills of which we hear so much are a new thing under the sun. Ills just as great, or greater, existed in the past; but they had not become living issues as they are to-day, because the public conscience was less sensitive, and most people regarded these things with indifference. But all this has been changed. Wrongs that once found no voice have become vocal in the Church, the market place, and the halls of legislation; a small army of trained experts are collecting and classifying the facts of social and industrial life as a foundation upon which future remedial action may proceed; preachers of righteousness are bringing the methods and maxims of business face to face with the Ten Commandments and the Sermon on the Mount. As a result of all this, social ills are being steadily repressed where they can not be altogether eliminated. Step by step the liquor traffic is restricted; social vice finds no open apologists, and the righteousness of one standard of morals for men and women gains new adherents every day. Cruelty to children, and even to animals, is punishable by statute; compulsory education is the law of the more advanced nations; enactments in the interests of labor are on almost every statute-book; the simple justice of a living wage (if we could only agree as to what that means!) for all who toil is generally admitted, and efforts to that end are steadily pursued. Best of all, the conviction grows that social ills are not incurable, and that a remedy will be found in the steady application of the laws of the kingdom of God to all the concerns of life. And what does all this indicate but the steady working of the gospel leaven in human society as Christ foretold it would, giving promise of a coming day when the whole mass will be leavened?

In dealing with any of the sociological problems of the day, a knowledge of the facts is indispensable.

Some one has said that the conditions of life of wasps and bees have been more thoroughly examined by Sir John Lubbock, and the habits of earthworms by Charles Darwin, than have the conditions of life of the common people. Such a reproach is scarcely true to-day. A search-light of intense power has been turned not only upon the slums of great cities, where the vicious and the criminal congregate, but also upon the homes—if they deserve the name—of the very poor, and such works as General Booth's "In Darkest England" and Mr. Charles Booth's "Life and Labor of the People"[1] have come as a revelation, dispelling much of the ignorance that once existed. That such books should come as a "revelation" is the strangest and saddest thing about it all. How could such a state of things exist, one might ask, and yet multitudes of Christian people in the same city be ignorant of the fact? Was it because, as of old, the priest and the Levite "passed by on the other side," and that only here and there was there a "Samaritan" who had time or

---

[1] The book which Mr. Charles Booth (no connection of the General, I believe) has given to the world is not the result of a hasty run through the slums. On the contrary, he and his associates determined to get to the bottom of the whole question. They went over a large part of East London "mile by mile, street by street, house by house, and room by room"; and their work is characterized by the impartiality of jurists and the accuracy of mathematicians. If it be said that these investigations refer only to the city of London, the obvious reply is that social problems are substantially the same everywhere, differing in degree rather than in kind.

inclination to turn aside to raise the fallen and pour a little oil and wine into wounds that were gaping wide? Perhaps so; or perhaps it was only that, beyond a vague surface notion that something was wrong, very few had any knowledge of the real facts in the case. To-day no such ignorance can be pleaded. Society's festering wounds have been laid bare in the light of the sun; and if the Church of God comes not to pour in the oil and the wine, it will go far to justify the reproach of a labor leader in England: "Shame, a thousand times shame, upon so feeble a religion as that which can tolerate the awful social life which exists in London to-day!" But religion—true religion—does not "tolerate" it in London or anywhere else, and religion must work with both hands to remove the reproach where it even seems to exist.

There is not much room for complaint in these days that the poor or the toilers are without a voice to tell their wrongs.[1] Ten thousand voices are clamoring on this one subject, and the voices have every variety of tone. We hear the moan or still more bitter cry of those who suffer, they scarcely know why; we hear the warning voice of those who have been behind the

---

[1] Sixty years ago Carlyle wrote: "How inexpressibly useful were a genuine understanding by the upper classes of society what it is that the under classes intrinsically mean; a clear interpretation of the thought which at heart torments these wild inarticulate souls, struggling there with inarticulate uproar, like dumb creatures in pain, unable to speak out what is in them!"

scenes, and who see in the struggling masses forces that threaten the civilization of the future; we hear the earnest appeals of those who would fain arouse the Church of God to grapple with the problems of the hour. Anon we hear the rasping tones of the professional agitator, whose delight it is to set class against class and interest against interest, and to keep alive the discontent out of which he makes his living or gains his notoriety; while from across the sea, and even in some cities of this continent, is heard the insane shriek of the anarchist, whose cry, when interpreted, means, "Back from cosmos to chaos!" To comprehend the meaning of all this confused uproar may not be easy; but one thing is clear: discontent so deep and widespread must have its source in some real trouble which, if we could but reach it, would suggest some remedy. It is not enough to say, amid the turmoil, that the great toiling, struggling, sweating masses don't know what they want. Of some of them it is true; of many of them it is partly true; of all of them it once was true, say in Carlyle's day, but not now. Be that as it may, it is the duty of the Church of God to find out what they want, and, so far as the wants are legitimate, help to supply them.

In these days numerous remedies for our social ills are persistently advertised. Our social "medicine men," like their patent-medicine prototypes, paint the diseases of the body politic in the darkest colors, and portray a condition of ideal health in hues superlatively bright; but whether any one of the advertised nostrums will prove to be the bridge over which a socially invalided race will pass from disease to health, can be determined only when the experiment is tried. I cherish an unwavering belief that better social conditions will prevail in the not distant future, but I also believe that this can be brought about only in so far as men are animated by the spirit and governed by the precepts of Jesus the Christ. We can have better social conditions only when we have better men, and the only way that has yet been discovered of making better men is the transforming power of the Spirit of God. The world has yet to learn that the root of all social ills is in man himself and not in his environments, and then it will be seen that the teachings of Jesus Christ embody the soundest philosophy and the most exact science. See how, in a single sentence, he cleaves his way to the very heart of this matter as with the stroke of a two-edged sword: "Either make the tree good, and its fruit good; or make the tree corrupt, and its fruit corrupt: for the tree is known by its fruit."[1] Neither in social life nor anywhere else "do men gather grapes from thorns, or figs of thistles."[2]

Not a few students of social and political problems write and speak of human laws and institutions as though they were automata, working by virtue of some inherent mechanism. But a law or an institution

---

[1] Matthew xii. 33. [2] Matthew vii. 16.

in itself is nothing, and it can do nothing save as it is controlled and operated by human intelligence. An imperfect institution controlled and operated by good men will work better than an ideal institution controlled by bad men. Slavery, in the hands of humane and upright men, will work better than liberty administered by Judge Lynch. Despotism, in the hands of a truly humane and upright ruler, with like-minded subordinates, will conserve the interests of the people better than an ideal democracy whose leaders are vicious and corrupt. I hold, therefore, that far more is accomplished by steady and continuous efforts to increase the number of humane and righteous men than by perpetual tinkering at laws and institutions without concerning ourselves as to the character of the men by whom they are to be administered; more especially as an increase of humane and righteous men is the surest and quickest way of improving laws and institutions that are imperfect, and reforming those that are bad. It can not be too often repeated that the laws and institutions which obtain in any self-governing community represent, approximately, the average of intelligence and morality in that community, and reforms will not do more than keep even pace with the moral growth of the people. Without expressing the slightest opinion as to the merits of different systems of government, it may be instructive to remember that France tried to force on republicanism before a real republican was born, and the reign of terror is history's significant warning to men not to repeat experiments of that kind prematurely. Assuming that there may be some degree of truth in the theory of evolution, it will be well to remember that we cannot safely force the pace by modern appliances. Evolution will take its time, no matter how impatient we may be.

If sociology is what Joseph Cook defines it to be, "the science, philosophy, and art of human welfare in life and death, and beyond death," the vastness of its scope might well deter one from any attempt to master it. Nor is the outlook more encouraging if we adopt Professor Ely's definition that sociology is the group name of the social sciences that relate to language, art, education, religion, family life, society life, political life, economic life.[1] Professor Herron is more terse and lucid when he calls it "the science of right human relations";[2] and so is Dr. Washington Gladden, who calls it "the science of human welfare."[3] But something different is wanted to express the conception of what is now called Christian sociology, or the application of the law of Christ to the solution of social problems. Its object, as expressed in the principles of the American Institute of Christian Sociology, is "to present Christ as the living Master and King of men, and his kingdom as the complete ideal of human society to be realized on earth"; but in doing this we

---

[1] "Outlines of Economics," pp. 81, 82.
[2] "Christianity Practically Applied," I., p. 458.
[3] "Applied Christianity," p. 221.

need not go beyond the plain teaching of the New Testament, especially of the Gospels. That Jesus contemplated an ideal state of society as the outcome of his kingdom among men admits, I think, of no dispute, and it is the vision of such a society, dim and distorted as it often is, that is stirring men's souls with a vague unrest. Society, as a whole, is yet very far from the gospel ideal, because as yet the scope of the gospel is imperfectly apprehended by the masses, and even the Church cannot be said to have realized all that Christ intended his kingdom to be. Perhaps this is why men in their blindness and impatience are preaching industrial and social revolutions to be brought about not by moral and spiritual forces, which is Christ's plan, but by compulsion, by confiscation, by robbery.

Those who may take the trouble to read these lectures are asked to remember that they have been prepared in such fragments of time as could be snatched from pressing duties of another kind, and may be lacking alike in logical arrangement and literary finish. They are, to say the least, far short of the author's own ideal of what the occasion demanded; but he had to content himself with a simple presentation of facts and inferences touching social duties and relationships that might show their intimate connection with the laws of the divine kingdom which God is establishing in the world. In all that is said there is an avoidance of mere declamation and of all appeals to passion or prejudice, keeping in mind the saying of the apostle:

"I speak as to wise men; judge ye what I say." It is quite possible that some of my views will be regarded as antiquated, if not obsolete. There are men who have gained considerable reputation in the domain of physical research who regard with ill-concealed impatience any hint of a belief that there is a God who still lives and reigns, as being altogether opposed to modern discoveries and advanced thought; but I have lived long enough to be convinced that not a little of what passes current as modern and advanced thought is only a revival of very ancient errors, and that men who have spent their lives in the study of the physical sciences are not the best qualified to pass judgment in the higher realm of spiritual beliefs. A case in point is that of the late Charles Darwin, who admitted toward the close of his life the effect upon his own singularly clear and powerful mind of exclusive devotion to a purely physical pursuit, in rendering him insensible to the whole class of conceptions which belong to the spiritual realm. But if in spite of warnings like these the conception of a divine kingdom in the earth, planned by divine wisdom and carried to its consummation by divine power, be still regarded as the dream of an enthusiast rather than the sober belief of a rational man, I must content myself to be even as "the voice of one crying in the wilderness," sustained only by the conviction that the cry repeats in its every tone the spirit of the ancient message: "Prepare ye the way of the Lord!"

LECTURE I.

THE KINGDOM OF GOD IN CONCEPTION AND OUTLINE.

"Not only philosophy and the so-called gnosis, but also the Scriptures, recognize and avow a divine ideal world to which the actual world stands related as the historical development of an eternal conception. (Delitzsch, "Biblische Psychologie," p. 23; quoted by Dr. Charles Hodge, "Systematic Theology," Vol. II., p. 66, English edition.)

"The sovereign people must not be sovereignless, but their only possible Sovereign is the God who is Lord of the conscience. His is the only voice that can still the noise of the passions and the tumult of the interests." (A. M. Fairbairn, D.D., "Religion in History," p. 61.)

"And in the days of these kings shall the God of heaven set up a kingdom, which shall never be destroyed: nor shall the sovereignty thereof be left to another people; but it shall break in pieces and consume all these kingdoms, and it shall stand forever." (Dan. ii. 44.)

"Any social order must stand in some veritable connection with the higher law of heaven. If it would be true and permanent, it must recognize the presence and power of the living God." (A. Scott Matheson, "The Church and Social Problems," p. 346.)

I.

PRELUDE.—SEARCHING FOR A CLUE.

IN the investigation of many important subjects some propositions have to be assumed, at least for a time. This may give to arguments the appearance of mere dogmatic statements that are not yet proved, and may even be incapable of proof. But such an objection has weight only in regard to the initial stage of a discussion. As the investigation proceeds the assumptions may be either verified or disproved, and only such as are verified can be retained. At the start certain assumptions may be necessary as a working hypothesis, if nothing more; later on they may be dispensed with, and their places supplied by conclusions based upon substantial evidence.

In attempting to show that from the beginning it has been the purpose of Almighty God to establish in this world a kingdom of truth and righteousness, and to present, if only in faint outline, the salient features of that kingdom, my arguments must be drawn chiefly from that Book which Christians call the Word of God. I will assume, for the time being, the trustworthiness of that Book as a revelation of the mind and will of God concerning the human race; that its history is reliable touching those occurrences of which it professes to give an account; that its prophetic announcements have in them the elements of "foretelling" as well as "forthtelling," and may be trusted at least to the full extent to which they have been fulfilled in history; and that its ethical teaching is along lines which tend to the highest development and greatest good of mankind. As we proceed it will be seen how far these assumptions are valid, or whether some or all of them must be abandoned as untenable.

In approaching the Scriptures, and especially those portions which speak of the beginnings of things, we should move with caution and interpret without dogmatism. The meaning we extract from a given passage is often colored by preconceived opinions. It is quite possible to deceive ourselves with the belief that we are developing the true meaning of the Scriptures when in fact we are simply bringing to light some notion which, all unconsciously perhaps, we had previously hidden there. This appears in the writings of two widely diverging schools of interpretation. It is found among those who adhere to the barest literalism in the interpretation of even highly figurative passages, and it is found in a more marked degree among those who are perpetually finding some mystical meaning hidden beneath the plainest statement of facts.

This difficulty has arisen, in part at least, from adopting the theory of verbal inspiration. This theory has never been very clearly defined, nor has it ever been expressly adopted, as far as I know, by any branch of the Christian Church; but in some form or other it has been widely prevalent, and in its logical outcome has presented many openings of which skeptics of all classes have not been slow to avail themselves. A conspicuous example of this is found in some of the writings of the late Professor Huxley.[1] Incautious statements of Christian apologists, apparently involving the position that Christianity is founded upon a series of events recorded in our sacred books, which events must have happened exactly as they are declared to have happened, the words being interpreted in the most literal way, have been seized by the Professor with avidity, distorted and made ridiculous, as is the fashion of his class, and then on the ground of these crude and even absurd interpretations he assails alike the Mosaic

---

[1] "Lights of the Church and the Light of Science."

cosmogony and the gospel narratives, relegating the creation, the fall, the flood, the call of Abraham, the whole Messianic doctrine, and the New Testament miracles to the same category as the Greek myths or the Roman legends. It will be seen, therefore, how important it is that we endeavor to hold an even balance between that extreme literalism which allows no room for the use of metaphor or poetic representation, and the vague mysticism which, in its anxiety to spiritualize every statement, robs plain words of their obvious meaning, and lands us among shifting quicksands where safe footing cannot be found.

It scarcely needs to be said that any theory of the universe, or of the history and destiny of the human race, which includes God and his purpose as chief factors is sure to meet with sturdy opposition; but the form of opposition changes as the years go by. The old argument drawn from the insignificance of this earth as compared with the rest of the universe, or even the rest of the solar system of which it forms a part, and how unlikely it is that it would be chosen as the theater of a divine drama lasting as time and comprehensive as the thought of God, is now seen to be inconclusive and even childish. If the universe is the outcome of intelligence, behind it there must be plan and purpose, not only for the universe as a whole, but for each separate part, and into the whole the parts must fit with perfect adjustment, otherwise the result will be confusion and disaster. Each creative thought of God must find embodiment sometime and somewhere in time and space, and if in the instances now under consideration that somewhere is but an outlying orb of minute dimensions, and the sometime a mere fragment of duration, yet that orb is an integral part of an illimitable universe, and that fragment belongs to an eternity that saw no beginning and will see no end. Physical bigness is not essential to the display of grand conceptions. The microscope, no less than the telescope, gives evidence of far-reaching plan and purpose, and divine wisdom is seen in the infinitely minute as clearly as in the in. finitely vast.

In the domain of natural science, and even of sciology, we find here and there some islets of knowledge surrounded by a vast ocean of ignorance. The known is so small compared with the unknown that Sir Isaac Newton's famous saying, in which he compares himself to a child at the seashore, gathering a few shells brighter than the rest, while the great ocean of truth lay before him unsounded and unexplored, is felt to be no exaggeration. If an explanation is asked of this paucity of results as compared with the expenditure of effort, it is not to be found in the exceptional difficulty of the problems themselves, nor yet in the insufficiency of the human mind to grapple with them, but rather in the fact that at the first students were under the necessity of studying the subjects without any guiding principle, hoping by the slow and painful accumulation of facts to reach some generalization that might be expressed in terms of universal application. Facts were always plentiful enough, but often it has been only after centuries of patient investigation that some underlying principle is discovered which unites and correlates the heterogeneous and seemingly discordant facts, so that they fall obediently into line under the sway of universal law.

In attempting a solution of the complex social problems that meet us at every turn, it becomes us to proceed with caution, for the field is strewn with dead issues and fragments of exploded theories, through which it is difficult to find one's way. Indeed, it will be impossible unless we can find an absolutely trustworthy clue. And although such a discovery may seem very doubtful to those whose search has resulted only in successive disappointments, yet he would be a bold man who would affirm that such a clue cannot be found. There was a time when the problem of the solar system was surrounded by difficulties quite as great as those which surround the sociological problems of to-day. In the nature of the case an *a priori* clue was out of the question. It was only by the slow accumulation of facts, and the testing and rejection of many theories, that the law of planetary motion could be discovered; but, once discovered, it furnished a clue whereby students of the future might find their way, safely and surely, through the intricate mazes of planetary and stellar motion throughout the whole universe.

There is this difference, however, in the two cases: In the search for physical laws the student is dealing, for the most part, with fixed and invariable quantities, and his mathematical or other signs have always and everywhere the same values; but in the search for laws that may underlie our sociological problems, he is dealing with forces which appear to be neither fixed nor invariable. He has to reckon with an entirely new factor. Human nature, with all its complex forces —moral, intellectual, and social—constitutes the chief part of the problem, and increases immensely the difficulty of solution. In other words, the student is no longer dealing with inert matter and the laws of motion and gravitation, which are always and everywhere the same; he has entered an entirely different realm, where the human mind, with its endless speculations, and human volition, with its practically unlimited power of choosing, have to be taken into account. In astronomical science it is very easy to measure the direction and intensity of all the forces that act upon the heavenly bodies, and to predict the result with absolute certainty; but who can catalogue the thousand and one influences of passion and prejudice, of interest and pleasure, of judgment and conscience, of volition and choice, which sway human actions, or predict the result of their ever-varying forces?

And yet if it be true that law is everywhere; if it be true that natural laws in their last analysis are simple as axioms and clear as the light; if it be true, as science seems to teach, that all power is one and comes from one source—it would be strange to the last degree if law should reign in the lower but not in the higher realm, or that law in that higher realm should be less clear and simple than the laws which pertain to the physical universe. There may be some who in a matter of this kind think with Tennyson that

> " We have but faith, we cannot know,
> For knowledge is of things we see ";

but that has been just as true in the realm of physical research as in the higher realm of mind. In astronomical science the laws of motion and gravitation were matter of faith before their existence was demonstrated or their universality revealed, just as a Western Hemisphere was matter of faith to Columbus before one of his ships left the coast of Spain. And it is my belief, reasoning not alone from analogy, that, underlying the swirl of that seething vortex we call society, there are laws that will account for all its movements, even the most erratic, and from which results may be predicted with at least moral certainty.

When Kepler, after long and patient investigation, found a clue which solved the problem of the movements of the heavenly bodies, he fell upon his knees and cried in solemn rapture, "Almighty God, I think thy thoughts after thee!" And if in tracing the conception and development of a divine kingdom among men we find a clue which solves otherwise insoluble problems; which guides us safely and surely through the mazes of human history—the growth and decay of empires, the rise and fall of dynasties, the shock of contending armies, the entanglements of statecraft, the heavings of social unrest, the awful problems of sin and suffering—until we emerge into the peace and glory of a never-ending kingdom, where human wrongs are righted, and human relationships are adjusted on a basis of eternal righteousness, we too may exclaim in solemn rapture, "Almighty God, we think thy thoughts after thee!"

Every student knows what an immense advantage is gained if he can begin the investigation of any branch of science with a knowledge of its underlying principles or laws, by the application of which each problem can be solved as it arises. And this, I submit, is the case when sociological problems are studied in the light of the great laws of the kingdom of God. He who confronts the complex and intricate problems which crowd the domain of man's social relations with no other guide than some theory that has been reasoned upward from amid the strife and clamor of human interests and passions is like one who wanders in the mazes of a labyrinth with no certain clue to guide his steps. Here and there he grasps what seems to be a clue, but finds it to be only a broken thread dropped by some one as bewildered as himself. Perplexed and almost despairing, what wonder if he abandons the task as one beyond human skill, and is ready to conclude that man is the victim of some malignant power from whom there is no escape; that the God in whom he was once taught to believe as the loving Father of men is, after all, only a sort of sculptured deity, who sits behind an impenetrable veil of second causes, " clutching in his cold metallic fingers iron bands of law," and gazing forth, with stony, Sphinx-like eyes, upon human souls that sin and suffer and human hearts that break.

But if human life in the aggregate of its problems is the hopeless labyrinth that some find it to be, it is past belief that it can be the result either of accident or malignant design, and the root of the difficulty must be sought in faulty methods of interpretation rather than in the facts which they seek to interpret. Doubtless there are some who still worship the great goddess Fortuity, and think that man is the sport of circumstance or the slave of fate; but they judge more truly who teach that the Maker of the universe and of all that it contains is neither a blind force nor a cold abstraction, but a living God whose mighty hand upholds all worlds, yet wipes the tear from sorrow's cheek; whose eye surveys the utmost limits of creation, yet notes the sparrow's fall; whose ear drinks in the melody of rolling spheres, yet catches the faintest whisper from the heart of trouble, and hears even the young ravens when they cry. Doubtless we are under law, and we rejoice that it is so. The universe is not left to the mercy of lawless chance. But law itself is subject to love, and the fountain of law is not a hard, stern necessity, but a loving Heart that beats in sympathy with man's highest aspirations, and cherishes a tender pity for human griefs and fears. And law itself is not a pitiless Juggernaut, remorselessly crushing whatever comes in its way; it is simply the living and loving God in action, working out the great plan and purpose of his kingdom, the final outcome of which shall be "glory to God in the highest, and on earth—peace."

LECTURE I.—THE KINGDOM OF GOD IN CONCEPTION AND OUTLINE.

In searching for a rational interpretation of the universe, or of this world as it actually exists, certain postulates seem to be inevitable. That the material universe can be eternal belongs to the class of unthinkable propositions. It must have had a beginning, and it is probable, to say the least, that it will have an end. Equally unthinkable is the proposition that the universe is self-evolved—that it is the cause of its own existence.

CONCEPTION AND OUTLINE. 15

The absurdity of such a proposition is self-evident, and shows that an atheistic conception of the universe is altogether inadmissible. A healthy human mind is so constituted that it demands an adequate cause for whatever is. It affirms that back of all phenomena—back of everything that we see or know—there must be power guided by intelligence, and both must belong to the realm of the infinite. In other words, infinite power and infinite intelligence are postulates necessary to a rational conception of the universe.

A second postulate is that the universe and all it includes is the outcome of a divine plan and purpose; for creation and providence are not a mere succession of unrelated occurrences: each event is a necessary part of a plan which began before time was, and will reach through the ages when time, as we understand the word, shall cease to be. Now a plan is a mental conception with reference to the future, and in the nature of things must precede its embodiment in visible form. We may infer, therefore, that the plan of the kingdom of God was a conception in the mind of its author long before it began to take shape as an actuality. And if it be true that God has in any way revealed himself to men, it would be reasonable to expect that the nature and purpose of this kingdom will be outlined at least in that revelation. Let any one, having this thought in mind, read again the Old Testament Scriptures, and he will be surprised to find how abundantly the thought is confirmed. He will be convinced that from the beginning it has been God's purpose to set up in this world a kingdom of righteousness and peace that shall eventually subdue all other kingdoms, and fill the whole earth with the glory of God.

Turning now to that record which we justly call a divine revelation, we are met, first of all, by a statement of the origin of things: "In the beginning God created the heaven and the earth." It is worthy of remark that in all the researches of scientists in modern times nothing has been discovered which even modifies this opening sentence of Genesis. All are agreed that there must have been a "beginning," and as the Scriptures say nothing as to the length of time that has elapsed since that beginning, there can be no chronological dispute in the case. As the design of revelation is to make known God's purpose concerning the human race, it is reasonable that it should begin with the story of creation, which serves as a background, throwing into strong relief the details of the picture as they are successively outlined.

Following the statement as to the origin of the heaven and the earth, there is a brief record of the successive steps whereby this earth was fitted to become the abode of a race of beings a little lower than the angels, but inconceivably higher than the brutes; and that part of the record ends with the appearance of the human race, as we know it, upon the stage. Materialistic evolution would dispute with us here, and contend that man had his real origin millions of ages earlier, in the lowest form of animated existence, and that his present condition is the result of a gradual evolution, modified by environment and natural selection, and also by the struggle for existence. But with a preadamite race, if such ever existed, we are not concerned, for the preadamite man, as sketched by the evolutionist, has nothing distinctively human about him. All we are concerned with is the fact that the intellectual, moral, and social history of the race begins with Adam and Eve. Only once since the beginning have human beings, possessed of intellectual and moral powers, appeared upon the scene, and it seems reasonable to conclude that these powers are a direct communication or gift from the Creator of all, rather than the result of evolution from a substance in which they did not originally inhere.

In close association with the origin of the race we find the institution of the home, based upon monogamous marriage, the union of one man with one woman, which is God's ideal of the family relation.[1] And this ideal is reaffirmed by Jesus in the most emphatic manner.[2] He explicitly condemns the practice of divorce for trifling causes as an infraction of the primal law, and recognizes only one ground on which it can be justified. The shifting of moral standards in regard to this matter is an ominous sign of the times, for no worse danger can threaten society than a blow aimed at the integrity of the home. The kingdom of God at its very inception recognized the sacredness of the marriage relation, and so long as the Church remains true to its King and its mission it must resolutely oppose every attempt to lower the standard of New Testament morality touching marriage and divorce. Society needs a moral tonic on this question, and I know of nothing better than a faithful inculcation of the gospel law of marriage.

Just at this stage, and while the first features of the kingdom of God were being faintly outlined, a terrible catastrophe intervened: "Sin entered into the world, and death through sin," changing

---

[1] Genesis ii. 24. [2] Matthew xix. 3-9.

at once man's moral relation to his Maker, and introducing an entirely new factor into human history. Many attempts have been made to explain away this sad fact, apparently for no better reason than that it conflicts with certain modern theories of the universe and of man. But if the fact of a great moral catastrophe, at the very beginning of human history, stands in the way of a consistent theory of evolution, it is time that the theory was so modified as to conform to the fact; for the fact remains, let evolutionists say what they will. Coleridge summed up the whole situation in a single sentence when he wrote: "A fall of some sort or other . . . is the fundamental postulate of the moral history of man." [1]

The point that chiefly concerns us here is that all conceptions of a kingdom of righteousness in this world are necessarily modified by this new fact in the history of the human race. Fallen and sinful beings cannot be dealt with in the same way as if they were righteous. It is no longer the question of a kingdom naturally unfolding in a congenial environment, where everything is favorable to its growth, but of a kingdom placed in a hostile environment, winning its way against oppo-

---

[1] *Table Talk*, May 1, 1830.

sing forces of the most formidable kind. But if a kingdom of righteousness is to be perpetuated under such circumstances, it is clear that it must contain some provision for dealing with sinful men whereby past sins may be forgiven and sinful dispositions and tendencies be completely eradicated; for unless there be some method whereby man may be reconciled to God, how can the kingdom of this world ever become the kingdom of our Lord and his Christ? It is not at all surprising, therefore, that almost immediately following the record of man's revolt we have intimations of the institution of sacrifice. As to how sacrifice first came to be practiced the Scriptures are silent, but when we find that it was observed by a member of the first family of mankind [1] we can scarcely doubt that its origin was divine; and this view is confirmed when we see that from the beginning the practice was characteristic of those who were called the sons of God as distinguished from those who were known as the children of men. Of the development of this practice, and its incorporation as a fundamental part of the religious system of the Hebrews, it is unnecessary to speak further than to say that the kingdom of God in a fallen

---

[1] Genesis iv. 4.

world was manifestly founded on vicarious sacrifice—the inscrutable principle of a life for a life.

Notwithstanding the fact that man had revolted, it is clear that intercourse between him and his Maker was not entirely suspended. The story of the cherubim and the flaming sword at the gateway of Eden,[1] taken in connection with the early institution of sacrifice, shows conclusively that a relation of some kind existed; but soon we come upon a new feature in the outlining of the kingdom, when God established covenant relations with man.[2] The overthrow of the primeval race by a flood of waters manifested in the most unmistakable way God's righteous displeasure with sin, making a perpetual distinction between him that serveth God and him that serveth him not; and now God enters into covenant with the head and representative of a new race,[3] selecting the rainbow[4] as the token thereof, a sure pledge that so long as the laws of nature continued to operate the earth should no more be destroyed by a flood.

The story of Babel has an interest, in connection with this discussion, as an incipient and premature endeavor on the part of man to found a

---

[1] Genesis iii. 24.
[2] Genesis vi. 18; ix. 12-16; xv. 18.
[3] Genesis ix. 8-10.
[4] Genesis ix. 13.

universal kingdom.[1] But it was an attempt that crossed the purpose of Almighty God, and he frustrated it by confounding the speech of the people and scattering them abroad upon the face of the earth.[2] This was the first, but it was not the last attempt of the kind. Babylon, Assyria, Greece, and Rome were all attempts in the same direction; but the history of all these nations serves to show that kingdoms built on selfishness and sustained by force are doomed to fall, for they have in themselves the seeds of their own destruction. Only that which is based on truth and righteousness, and is sustained by love and justice, can ultimately prevail in a universe where God rules. Nor is the Babel story without its analogue in the intellectual realm. The wise ones of this world—the scholars, the philosophers, the scientists, and sometimes the theologians — have tried a similar experiment. They have set themselves to build out of natural laws and human speculations "a tower, whose top should reach unto heaven," and overlook in its pride the very temple of God; but again and again has the old result followed: God has "confounded their speech," so that they have "left off to build," at least, upon the old lines.

---

[1] Genesis xi. 4.   [2] Genesis xi. 7, 8.

In the call of Abraham out of Ur of the Chaldees we have the first direct step in the founding of the kingdom of God in the earth; and in the few incidents recorded of the Father of the faithful we have some indications of what the future kingdom was to be. Its citizens were to be a chosen people, called out from among the nations, and who would be willing at the command of God to forsake, if needs be, both country and kindred that they might be true to the new vocation. In a sense they were to be in the world but not of it. For the time being they were to have no possession in the land of Canaan. Dwelling in tents, they sojourned there for a season, looking by faith "for the city which hath the foundations, whose architect and maker is God."[1]

There are many incidents in the life of Abraham and his immediate descendants that are interesting because they afford some hints of God's purpose touching his kingdom, but upon these we need not dwell. Let it suffice to call to remembrance the first definite fulfillment of the promise of God in the birth of Isaac, pledge of the promised seed who was yet to come; the renewal of the covenant on various occasions, with intimations of a wider

---

[1] Hebrews xi. 10.

purpose in the declaration that in the promised seed all nations of the earth should be blessed; the trial of Abraham's faith, and the opportunity it afforded for teaching Abraham, and through him the world, that the principle of atonement lay at the very basis of the divine kingdom, and that God himself would provide a lamb for an offering; the checkered career of Jacob, and the transformation wrought in the man on the memorable night when he wrestled with the Angel of the Covenant, foreshadowing the great gospel doctrine of a spiritual regeneration; the selling of Joseph into Egypt, another link in the chain of preparatory providences; the going down of Jacob and his household into Egypt, and his death in the land of strangers; the long and painful bondage of his descendants; the sending forth of a great deliverer; the signs and mighty wonders by which the deliverance of the people was accomplished; the institution of the Passover; the march out of Egypt; the triumphant passage of the Red Sea; the long encampment before the mount, where God came down in majesty to proclaim his law and establish his kingdom—all these belong to the preparatory stage, but, like the unrolling of a magnificent panorama, they show the successive steps which led up to the founding of the theocracy, the kingdom of God among men.

The polity of the kingdom of God, as outlined in the laws of the Hebrew commonwealth, was in marked contrast with the customs of other nations, and plainly indicated that it was God's purpose to separate his chosen people completely from the nations that were round about them. The foundation truth of their religion was expressed in the phrase, "Hear, O Israel: The Lord our God is one Lord,"[1] and was a standing protest against the polytheistic idolatry of all surrounding nations. In an age when polytheism was universal, and in Egypt had reached its most degrading forms, the assertion of the divine unity, as a fundamental principle of the Mosaic code, is one of the most remarkable facts in human history, and of itself goes far to establish the claim that that code was a veritable revelation from heaven. Indeed, it may be said that the great truth that there is but one God, whose nature is holy and whose will is the sole standard of right, shaped and inspired the whole Hebrew polity, and constituted the broad line of demarcation between them and the rest of the world; thus bringing into view the conception of a kingdom in the world but not of it, type of that more perfect kingdom to be established

---

[1] Deuteronomy vi. 4.

when the dispensation of the law should pass to make way for the dispensation of truth and grace.

It is noteworthy that that root or summary of the divine law which we call the Decalogue stands in the very forefront of the Mosaic code. With the exception of the institution of the Passover, and the law of the redemption of the firstborn, there is nothing in that code which precedes it in point of time, and nothing that approaches it in point of importance. Among human codes of ancient or modern times there is nothing with which it can be compared. The very best of them fall infinitely short of the moral grandeur, the comprehensive sweep, the searching incisive spirit of that law which was given to the world when "God spake all these words and said." Whatever may be true as to the date of other portions of the Pentateuch, no unprejudiced mind can doubt that this corner stone of the Hebrew commonwealth, this foundation of all enduring legislation from that day to this, belongs to the time of Moses and the exodus. And when we remember that this was the primary law of a people just escaped from centuries of bondage—a people without a religion, or a civil polity, or any social organization worthy of the name—the fact that they start upon their national career with a code in which, even under the intense search-light of modern criticism, no flaw has been discovered, stamps the whole with a divine impress, the very image and superscription of the Most High. Of the body of Levitical statutes which came after, it is not necessary to speak at large. They were fitted to the circumstances of an untrained people in the initial stages of their political and religious development, and when they had served their purpose they passed away; but the moral code, broad as human life and fitted to the wants of a race through all time, firm on its foundations as the mount where it was given, and like it rising in calm, undisturbed serenity above the lower ranges about it, still stands immovable, the one supreme standard of human conduct in all relationships, the divine ideal of what the laws of a state should be.

The immediate result of the promulgation of this law was the creation of a divine commonwealth, the segregation of a people with lofty aims and ideals, regarding themselves as in a peculiar sense the people of God, charged with an important mission as depositaries of a divine revelation. Of the part they were yet to play in the history of the world their leaders had no clear conception, and even their prophets may have been but dimly conscious of the far-reaching import of the messages they uttered. The Levitical economy, in its social and political aspects, was, for the most part, national and local, and even in its religious aspects did not possess the characteristics of a universal religion; but underlying all that was local, national, and temporary there was a substance that was both enduring and universal, and this substance remained when the old form had passed away. The relation of Christian civilization to the Hebrew code is the relation of the flower and the fruit to the root from which they spring. Christianity is not the law of Moses continued in the rigid outline of the letter; it is that law unfolded in its inner meaning and carried forward to its full logical and spiritual results; and it may be safely affirmed that " all that civilization has wrought for social good, for the marriage bond, for the ties of the family, for chastity, for honesty, for the safeguard of human life, for the right of property, the right of a good name, for the training of the man, the neighbor, the citizen, is but the ripe growth of this ancient Book, written in the morning of the world, which has entered into the conscience, the history of mankind." [1]

---

[1] E. A. Washburn, D.D., "The Social Law of God," p. 7.

At the time when the Israelites became firmly settled in Canaan, and for some three centuries later, certain features of the kingdom of God as established among them may be clearly traced. The government was a pure theocracy, God being recognized as sole Lawgiver and King. A casual reading of Exodus and Leviticus might lead to the conclusion that there was a fourfold code of laws —moral, religious, civil, and criminal—but a more careful reading shows that the three latter divisions, if they may be so called, had their root and source in the first, and that the whole constitutes one body of laws covering every relation of the citizen to God and his fellow-men. In part, as we have seen, these laws, in their literal form, were designed for a temporary purpose. In their minute details they were exactly suited to the earlier stages of the nation's development, for as yet the people could neither comprehend nor apply those great principles on which the whole economy of the kingdom was based. In the meantime the law was their schoolmaster until the fullness of the time when the newness of the spirit should replace the oldness of the letter.

The salient features of the kingdom of God, at this period, may be summed up as follows: 1. A chosen people, called out and separated from all other nations.[1] 2. The recognition of God as sole King and Head of the nation, and the repudiation of all government but his.[2] 3. The recognition of God's law as the ultimate standard of appeal touching religious duties, moral conduct, civic responsibilities, and social relationships.[3] 4. The recognition of God as absolute Proprietor, citizens of the kingdom being but stewards. This is indicated more especially in the laws respecting the redemption of the firstborn,[4] the payment of tithes,[5] and the surrender of property rights in the year of jubilee.[6] 5. A social system designed to prevent injustice and oppression, and to shield the poor and needy, the stranger and the fatherless.[7]

Such, in brief outline, was the kingdom of God as foreshadowed in the Jewish commonwealth; but it is abundantly clear that this was not to be a finality. It was but a shadow of something that

---

[1] Exodus vi. 7; Leviticus xx. 24.

[2] Nevertheless God foresaw that they would choose a King after they were settled in Canaan, and provision was made for this (Deut. xvii. 14, 15); but it was no part of his plan that they should do so (1 Sam. viii. 7).

[3] Numbers xv. 30, 31; Deuteronomy iv. 2.

[4] Exodus xiii. 2–13.

[5] Leviticus xxvii. 30–32.

[6] Leviticus xxv. 10–23, 39–41.

[7] Exodus xxii. 21–24; Leviticus xxiii. 22; xxv. 14.

was yet to come. The Hebrew polity was national, but it embodied principles that were of universal application. In its details of observance it was suited to the childhood of a people, but in its fundamental truths it was for all time and for all stages of development. The dispensation was temporary, but the truth was eternal. The Hebrew ritual has no authority now, but the great principles of the moral law stand unchanged and unrepealed. This becomes increasingly clear as we advance along the lines of historical development. The Hebrew polity, regarded from the standpoint of mere political sagacity, might be pronounced a failure; and had the purpose of God been limited to the political fortunes of that one nation, the polity might justly have been called a failure in the broadest sense; but in its conception the kingdom of God was far wider than national or race boundaries, and its development must run parallel with the lines of human progress down to the end of time.

If the divine polity seemed to fail in the case of the Hebrew people, it was not because of any inherent defect in the system itself, which was eminently suited to its purpose, but to the rebellious temper and spirit of the people, and their incurable tendencies toward idolatry. But even the seeming failure was overruled for good. The world was taught the great lesson that law can make nothing perfect; that it cannot of itself reach the seat of sin's inveterate disease, or rescue men from the bondage of their own corruptions. At best it is suited only to the earlier stages of spiritual development and can accomplish only a preparatory work. But the divine kingdom which law and prophecy foreshadowed was to be signalized by the bringing in of a better hope, the introduction of a new covenant, when God would put his laws into the hearts of men and write them, not as of yore on tables of stone, but in the minds of a willing people, and by the regenerating power of the Holy Spirit make obedience easy and self-surrender a delight. Even in times of greatest national abasement and disaster this vision of an ideal kingdom filled the prophets with a divine enthusiasm that no reverses could dampen or destroy. Through the gloom of the nation's darkest hour they saw the dawning of a better day, when "a King" should "reign in righteousness, and princes . . . rule in judgment";[1] and when "the earth" should "be filled with the knowledge of the glory of the Lord, as the waters cover

---

[1] Isaiah xxxii. 1.

the sea."[1] That day they might not live to see, but they knew that it would come, for the mouth of the Lord had spoken it.

But there came a time when the prophet's voice was hushed into silence and there was no open vision. The oracles of the heathen were dumb, and the heavens gave no sign. Slowly the centuries dragged their weary rounds, and it seemed as though God had forgotten the world he had made. But though men knew it not, God's purpose still lived, and just when the darkness was deepest the morning star of hope arose. In the silence of the world's midnight angel voices awoke the slumbering echoes with tidings of peace and joy to men. Zion's long captivity was ended, and the King was coming to his own. A thrill went through the nation like the pulsing tides of a new life. The prophetic impulse awoke again, and once more God "spake unto the fathers by the prophets." And while men looked and listened, marveling whereunto these things might grow, from the wilderness of Judea the message for which the world so long had waited rang out in joyous tones: "THE KINGDOM OF HEAVEN IS AT HAND."

---

[1] Hebrews ii. 14.

LECTURE II.

THE PRINCIPLES AND POLITY OF THE KINGDOM OF GOD.

"The principles of a reconstructed society are not yet understood, though the age is in a ferment of ideas about them. We have those principles wrapped up in our gospel of the kingdom of God, but they need to be mastered by the Church, freely discussed and fully wrought out, with the view of being taught to the people, and ultimately acted upon in the work of reform." (A. Scott Matheson, "The Church and Social Problems," p. 10.)

"Think not that I came to destroy the law and the prophets: I came not to destroy, but to fulfill. For verily I say unto you, Till heaven and earth pass away one jot or one tittle shall in no wise pass away from the law till all things be accomplished." (Matt. v. 17, 18.)

"My kingdom is not of this world: if my kingdom were of this world, then would my servants fight." (John xviii. 36.)

"The kingdom of God cometh not with observation: neither shall they say, Lo here; or, lo there! for, behold, the kingdom of God is within you." (Luke xvii. 20, 21.)

"'There is another King, one Jesus.' The safety of the State can be secured only in the way of humble and whole-souled loyalty to his person, and obedience to his law." (Prof. A. A. Hodge, "Popular Lectures on Theological Themes," p. 287.).

II.

PRELUDE.—THE RELATION OF THE KINGDOM OF GOD TO CIVIL GOVERNMENTS.

THIS is a subject of profound importance, involving the whole question of patriotism and the duties that grow out of it. In this connection I do not refer solely or even chiefly to the problem of Church and State as popularly understood. That is substantially a dead issue on this continent, at least in its ancient form; and if Christians to-day have any duty in that regard, it is to watch with jealous care against everything which might have a tendency to introduce the vicious principles of a political union between Church and State in lands now free from it, or to perpetuate the principle in lands where it still has a footing. Some may regard this word of warning as entirely unnecessary; but he who imagines that the only way in which the State—the kingdom of this world—can dominate the kingdom of God is by constituting the earthly ruler the head of the Church, as in England, or making the Church the mere tool of the State, as in Russia or Germany, shows that he has profited little by the lessons of history. And he has profited less who thinks that the danger lies all on that side. Immeasurably worse results have followed from the domination of the Church over the State than from the domination of the State over the Church.

In the primitive Church the sense of citizenship in the kingdom of God changed at once and forever the relation of believers to all earthly kingdoms, and to the laws and customs by which those kingdoms were governed. Believers were united to Christ and to each other by bonds stronger than those of nationality or even of kindred. They recognized each other as brethren in a sense that scarcely belongs to the word to-day. The duty of obedience to the civil authority under which they lived, in all things that could be rendered with a good conscience, was never disputed; nay, more, such obedience was required by the very laws of that heavenly kingdom of which they claimed to be citizens.[1] Cæsar was entitled to honor, custom, tribute [2]—everything which did not interfere with fealty to the divine law; but when the demands of the civil authority came into conflict with higher claims there was but one thing for the Christian believers to do, and that was to be loyal

---

[1] 1 Peter ii. 13-17; Romans xiii. 1-8.   [2] Matthew xxii. 21.

to Christ at all hazards, and then submit without murmuring to whatever penalty the civil power might inflict. They did not refuse to pay taxes, no matter how unjust or excessive; they did not refuse to pray for those in authority, although they were heathens, or even men of vicious lives. In a word they were "subject to every ordinance of man for the Lord's sake"; but if they were required, as was often the case, to burn but one grain of incense before the statue of Jupiter, or pour out one drop of wine as a libation to Venus or Diana, they would submit to the martyr's cross or to be thrown to wild beasts in the arena rather than obey.

In apostolic times, and for two centuries following, the line of cleavage between the kingdom of God and the kingdoms of this world was broad and distinct. The former was founded upon principles antagonistic to those of the latter, and between them there could be no compromise without damage to one or both. This mutual antagonism grew in part out of the widely different spirit which animated the two kingdoms, and in part out of their opposing polities. The whole spirit and constitution of the kingdom of God was an emphatic protest against the very things that were characteristic of the kingdoms of this world, namely, war, class distinctions, and Mammon worship, and moving on such lines collision was only a question of time. This was clearly perceived by the governments of this world, especially that of imperial Rome. It was not a mere question of rival religions. Had that been the case, there might have been no conflict, for Rome was tolerant of anything that did not challenge her supremacy, or interfere with her authority or system of government. Had it been only a question of a new religion, the Christians might have set up an image of Jesus and might have burned incense before it to their hearts' content; for what signified one god more or less to the haughty Roman whose Pantheon was crowded with gods from every nation? But a kingdom whose principles and polity antagonized the very foundations on which Roman power and government were built was a very different matter, and Rome's farseeing rulers quickly perceived that two such kingdoms could not exist side by side—one must give way before the other; and so Rome set herself, with steadfast purpose, to extirpate the new religion as a dangerous menace to the State.

It is necessary at this point to note an important distinction between two phrases which are almost identical in form but widely diverse in meaning. The first is the phrase, "the *kingdoms* of the world," or of "this world." It occurs very rarely in the Scriptures in the plural form, and where it occurs is to be understood in its obvious sense. The other phrase is, "the *kingdom* of the world," which occurs only in Revelation xi. 15, according to the revised translation, which is undoubtedly the correct one. As thus used the phrase has no reference to any political division of the earth's surface, nor to any form of government, but to that deep underlying spirit which permeates society everywhere; something invisible, intangible, yet wonderfully powerful; a spirit ever changing, and yet, in its last analysis, always the same. In Noah's time it was incarnated in violence; in Elijah's time in idolatry; in Christ's time in oppression of the poor; in our time in Mammon worship, which is the root of all evil. For want of a better name we call it the spirit of the age. Germans call it *Zeitgeist*, the "Time Spirit," or "Spirit of the Time," the intellectual and moral tendencies of an age or epoch. But the Scriptures have a more forceful word still. Paul personifies this spirit as "the god of this world," who "hath blinded the minds of the unbelieving," and again as "the prince of the power of the air, the spirit that now worketh in the children of disobedience."

But whatever be the name or nature of this intangible force, the result of its influence is to render the human soul insensible to the whole class of conceptions which belong to the spiritual realm. This is the foe with which the kingdom of God must ever be at war. With the governments of the nations, as such, it has no dispute. They are of this world, and the policy they pursue accords with that fact. Christ's kingdom is not of this world, and its policy is on different lines. If it collides with the policy of earthly kingdoms, it should never be on the ground of mere preference for one form of government rather than another, which is a matter with which a citizen of the kingdom of God has very little concern. His quarrel is not with human governments, but with "the kingdom of this world"—the mighty *Zeitgeist* of the ages. Against that he must maintain unceasing and relentless warfare. To overthrow this kingdom and set up the kingdom of God in its place has been the divine purpose through all the ages; but this result cannot be achieved by political agitation, much less by a social revolution brought about by political intrigues: it can be accomplished only by moral forces, by the universal spread and acceptance of the laws of the kingdom of God.

What, then, is or ought to be the relation of the

kingdom of God to human governments? In the days of primitive Christianity this question could have been answered more easily than now. Then human governments were distinctly and avowedly hostile to the new religion. The conflict of the Church was with an effete but bigoted Judaism on the one hand, and a dominant heathenism on the other, and there could not be a truce with either. The lines of separation were sharply drawn, and it was easy to see that the duty of Christians was to stand aloof and have no fellowship with the unfruitful works of darkness. But circumstances, we are told, have greatly changed. Among civilized nations, as a rule, Christianity is in the ascendant; nay, in some nations a form of Christianity has been adopted as the State religion; and in others it has so spread that they are called by many, in good faith, Christian nations. But in what sense is this true? Only in the sense that in those nations many persons profess the Christian religion, not in the sense that their governments are based either professedly or in fact on the principles of New Testament Christianity. To put it in another form, where is the government that is not based upon the very principles which Christ's kingdom came to antagonize—namely, brute force, class distinctions, and Mammon worship?

Doubtless it is true that circumstances have changed; but have they, in the matter now under consideration, changed for the better? I doubt it. In the days of primitive Christianity the rule was to render to Cæsar all honor and obedience that did not conflict with fidelity to Christ and his law, but now the rule seems to be to render to Christ all honor and obedience that does not interfere with loyalty to party, or with the customs and usages of the kingdom of this world; and this is excused or justified under the plea of patriotism, and by some is even called Christian patriotism. The term is a misnomer. Christian patriotism seeks first the kingdom of God and his righteousness; mere political patriotism seeks first the kingdom of this world and its advancement. We teach our children to love their country, and by implication to hate or despise every other; Christ taught his followers to love the whole world, and to hate no one. We teach the political brotherhood of a common nationality; Christ taught the universal brotherhood of man. The very best that a Christian can wish for his country is that Christ be received as Lord and Master, and his law applied to all the concerns of life, and he is the true patriot who has lived and labored with that end in view. The man who proposes anything lower than this as his ultimate aim is not a patriot but a partisan.

But has a Christian no duties as a citizen of an earthly kingdom? Doubtless he has, but always in subordination to his duty as a citizen of the kingdom of God. Or rather, let me say, he who is loyal, first of all, to Jesus Christ will be the best and most faithful citizen of the earthly kingdom in which he sojourns. Indeed, if all men were true Christians, the world could dispense almost with law and government as methods of force no longer needed. This is no mere guesswork. For the first three hundred years there was no crime in the Christian communities; but when they began to surrender the laws of Christ and to accept those of human governments instead, then crime began, and has continued ever since. The Christian's duty to the State is to uphold the authority of rulers in all lawful and just things, to obey every law and ordinance that can be obeyed with a good conscience toward God; but to oppose, steadily and resolutely, whatever conflicts with the principles of the kingdom of God, and to this end must keep himself free from party domination, and from all entangling alliances.

That the kingdom of God, as such, should form no alliance with the kingdoms of this world is an affirmation having all the force of an axiom. The sphere and functions of the two kingdoms are so entirely distinct that they cannot be merged, or even allied, without irreparable damage to the heavenly kingdom. The gulf which separates them was recognized in that saying of the Master, "Render therefore unto Cæsar the things which are Cæsar's; and unto God the things that are God's";[1] and so long as the Church kept that distinction in mind as the guiding star of her polity, her progress in the face of bitter hostility and tremendous odds was the marvel of the ages. But when she surrendered "the things that" were "God's" in exchange for the protection and patronage of the State, small marvel that she began to crave "the things that" were "Cæsar's," and became emphatically a kingdom of this world. The alliance of the kingdom of God with the kingdom of this world in the fourth century was a colossal mistake, from the effects of which it has not entirely escaped even to this day. It was the admission of a vicious principle which robbed the Church of her freedom and led to compromises of the most dangerous kind. When the Church became the ally of the State, Christ's laws regarding war, class

---

[1] Matthew xxii. 21.

distinctions, and property rights were virtually repudiated, and laws and customs of an opposite tendency were accepted in their stead. The Church had been founded on the principles of universal peace, universal brotherhood, and community rights; imperial Rome, like all human governments, was founded on military force, class privileges, and the domination of wealth. An alliance between two such kingdoms was unnatural, indeed impossible. Allies they could not long remain, for in the nature of things the one must dominate the other. The unalterable law of Christ's kingdom is: "Ye cannot serve God and mammon."[1] He does not merely appeal to the sense of right in his followers, saying, "Ye *ought not* to serve God and mammon," nor does he utter an imperative prohibition, "Ye *must not* serve God and mammon"; but he affirms a principle universally and absolutely true, "Ye *cannot* serve God and mammon."

The phrase "kingdom of God," or "kingdom of heaven," which is used to designate Christ's conception of an ideal human society, is one which at first thought suggests a form of government repugnant to modern notions of human

---

[1] Matthew vi. 24.

liberty and equality, and might be regarded by social *doctrinaires* as a retrograde rather than a progressive step; but when the nature of the divine kingdom is fully apprehended, not only as a spiritual force within men's souls, producing new affections and leading to new lines of action, but also as a philosophy of life covering all personal and social relations, we are brought face to face with the startling paradox that the kingdom of God, organized on lines not merely of kingship but of positive autocracy, where Christ is sole Lawgiver and King, is nevertheless the only perfect democracy which is possible to men; for no man is truly qualified for democratic self-government until he has become, in very deed and truth, a citizen of the kingdom of God.

There is another point touching the relation of Christians to human governments which should not be overlooked. In case of disputes arising in the Church, or of injury inflicted upon any of its members, the primitive Christians, as a rule, refused to seek redress in the civil courts, deeming such a course to be at variance with the very constitution of the kingdom of God. At Corinth it was different. There the practice continued for a time, but Paul sharply rebuked it, as well as the practice of setting those to judge who were of no account in the Church.[1] All things in the Church were to be judged by divine and not by human laws, which, in their very nature, flatly antagonized the laws of the kingdom of God. Thoughtful Christians clearly perceived that crime was largely the outcome of the false systems which human governments had established, and that to invoke the protection of human laws served only to perpetuate the evil. It was also perceived that if the laws of the divine kingdom were accepted and obeyed crime must cease. Where government by force is unnecessary there can be no treason; where class distinctions and privileges are unknown there will be neither jealousy nor envy; where human brotherhood is the rule there will be no war; and where property is not regarded as private possession, but is administered as a trust for the common good, there can be little temptation to dishonesty or fraud.

---

[1] 1 Corinthians vi. 1-8.

LECTURE II.—THE PRINCIPLES AND POLITY OF THE KINGDOM OF GOD.

In discussing the principles and polity of the kingdom of God it is necessary to bear in mind its twofold aspect: first, as an invisible spiritual force in the souls of men; and secondly, as a visible community, revealing itself as the outcome of that force. The first is the kingdom in its heavenward aspect, the enthronement of the living Christ in the heart, answering to that broad saying of Jesus: "Except a man be born from above,[1] he cannot see the kingdom of God."[2] The second is the kingdom in its earthward aspect, the kingdom actually existing as an organized community, in the world but not of it, yet touching all human interests and relationships, winning its way, not by revolution but by evolution, until "the kingdom of the world" becomes "the kingdom of our Lord, and of his Christ."[3]

Let us now try to ascertain, as clearly as we can, the principles on which the kingdom of God has been founded, and the polity by which its citizens are to be governed. It may be said in advance that in the Gospels we shall not find the principles of

---

[1] Marginal reading, Revised Version.
[2] John iii. 3.
[3] Revelation xi. 15.

the divine kingdom methodically arranged, paragraph by paragraph, like the written constitution of a modern state. On the contrary we shall find them only in detached sentences, in brief sayings, in parabolic illustrations, but none the less clear and authoritative on that account. In this respect there is a marked contrast between the Old Testament and the New. In the commonwealth and Church of the Hebrews the civil and religious polities are closely allied, and both find expression in the form of specific enactments; and as these were for the guidance of a people recently escaped from slavery, and, for the most part, ignorant of the first principles of religious truth or civil government, it was necessary that the laws should be at once comprehensive and minute, from the all-embracing principle of supreme love to God down to the most circumstantial details of civic duty or religious observance. At such a time, and among such a people, the conception of a spiritual kingdom, embracing the great principles of the fatherhood of God and the brotherhood of man, was scarcely possible, and it was necessary to place them under law as under a schoolmaster until, in the fullness of time, the letter should give place to the spirit, and men would learn that true citizenship in the kingdom meant also sonship with God.

Turning to the very foundation, what, first of all, is the charter of enfranchisement—the title by virtue of which men enter the kingdom of God? For if there is one truth concerning it which is clearer than another, it is this: that the boundaries of the kingdom of God as established by Jesus Christ are not conterminous with the human race, nor are men citizens thereof in virtue of their natural birth; but if they enter at all, it can be only by a spiritual regeneration wrought by the power of the Holy Spirit. Over the very portal of the kingdom this great truth is written plain for all men to see: "Except a man be born anew, he cannot see the kingdom of God."[1] When announcing this foundation law Jesus does not say, "Ye *may* be born again," or "Ye *ought* to be born again," but "Ye *must* be born again," and without this there is no entrance into the kingdom. The reason is plain: "That which is born of the flesh is flesh";[2] it belongs only to the kingdom of this world, a kingdom which is transient and will pass away; but "that which is born of the Spirit is spirit";[2] it belongs to a spiritual, and therefore an everlasting, kingdom. The law of regeneration is not a mere arbitrary condition of admission to the

---

[1] John iii. 3. [2] John iii. 6.

kingdom; neither is it the affirmation of a theological dogma, based upon a doctrine of total depravity; it is the simple statement of a fact universally and scientifically true, that a man can pass from that kingdom of the flesh wherein he was born into that spiritual kingdom which Christ has revealed, only by means of a new divine life imparted by the Spirit of God.

God's kingdom in the hearts of men is builded by the Holy Spirit, and man's interference mars instead of helping the work. All that man can do is to submit himself utterly to the control and guidance of those spiritual forces by which alone his nature can be renewed in righteousness. Of this renewal the final outcome is the heavenly state, and all that such a state implies may safely be left to Him who has gone to prepare a place for His people. But in the building up of the kingdom of God on earth, where so much is left to human effort, we must see to it that we are not turned aside by human plans, much less by the things of the kingdom of this world, but that we " make all things according to the pattern " that has been shown to us " in the mount."

A second principle which lies at the foundation of this kingdom is that of the fatherhood of God. But the fatherhood which Jesus taught is a different thing from the fatherhood portrayed in some of the erratic developments of modern theology. That God is the Father of all men in the sense of being their Creator is true,[1] but the inferences sometimes drawn from that truth are altogether misleading. Divine beneficence makes the "sun to rise on the evil and the good, and sendeth rain on the just and the unjust,"[2] but it does not follow that God makes no distinction between the two classes as regards their moral relation. As there is a broad distinction between the kingdom of God and the kingdom of this world, so in the nature of the case there must be between the subjects of these kingdoms. If it were otherwise—if there were no difference "between him that serveth God and him that serveth him not"[3]—there would be an utter confounding of all moral distinctions. We need only turn to the teaching of Jesus to see how distinct is the line of cleavage between the two classes. When certain of the Jews said, "We have one Father, even God, Jesus said unto them, If God were your Father, ye would love me."[4] And again: "Ye are of your father the devil, and the lusts of your father it is

---

[1] Malachi ii. 10.
[2] Matthew v. 45.
[3] Malachi iii. 18.
[4] John viii. 41, 42.

PRINCIPLES AND POLITY. 55

your will to do."[1] The point to be noted is that God is the Father of regenerate men in a sense in which he is not the Father of the unregenerate, and it is this which determines whether they are in the kingdom of God or not.

A third foundation principle is the kingship of Jesus Christ. If it be true that God has established, or is establishing, a kingdom in the earth, there must be rule and authority somewhere; and if that authority is to mean anything, there must be some name to which every knee shall bow in willing homage.[2] That it has been God's purpose from the beginning that this kingly power should be exercised by his only-begotten Son is perfectly clear. In the opening chapters of revelation there is reference to a coming seed of the woman who should lie in wait for the serpent's head.[3] In the last words of Jacob, as he lay upon his dying bed, a Person yet unseen and unknown is referred to as the Shiloh to whom is to be the gathering of the people.[4] Moses foresaw him as "a Star out of Jacob, and a Scepter . . . out of Israel," who should " break down all the sons of

---

[1] John viii. 44.
[2] Philippians ii. 10, 11.
[3] Genesis iii. 15. See marginal reading of Revised Version.
[4] Genesis xlix. 10.

tumult."[1] In the second Psalm God declares concerning this coming One, "I have set my King upon my holy hill of Zion"; and to this King, who is announced as the begotten Son of God, he promises to give "the nations for" an "inheritance," and the uttermost parts of the earth for a "possession."[2] Isaiah speaks of him as One on whose shoulders should be the government, and of the increase of whose government there should be no end.[3] Still more significant are the words of Daniel: "I saw in the night visions, and behold, there came with the clouds of heaven one like unto a son of man, and he came even to the ancient of days, and they brought him near before him. And there was given him dominion, and glory, and a kingdom, that all the peoples, nations, and languages should serve him: his dominion is an everlasting dominion, which shall not pass away, and his kingdom that which shall not be destroyed."[4]

In the New Testament Christ's kingly character is set forth with equal clearness. Thus the angel Gabriel, in announcing the Saviour's birth, declares: "He shall be great, and shall be called the Son of the Most High; and the Lord God

---

[1] Numbers xiv. 17.
[2] Psalm ii. 6–8.
[3] Isaiah ix. 6, 7.
[4] Daniel vii. 13, 14.

shall give unto him the throne of his father David, and he shall reign over the house of Jacob forever; and of his kingdom there shall be no end."[1] Much of Christ's teaching incidentally sets forth the same idea, for, although the kingdom is often the main subject of his parables, there can be no kingdom without a king, and there can be no doubt as to what king is meant.

A fourth foundation principle of the kingdom of God is the equality of all believers, and in this the true democracy of the kingdom appears. The whole spirit of the gospel is against those arbitrary distinctions which divide men into classes as they may be learned or ignorant, rich or poor, noble or plebeian.[2] The law of the kingdom recognizes only moral distinctions; all others are mere accidents, and in the nature of things cannot be permanent. On the other hand, the spirit of the gospel is equally opposed to that spurious equality that has been so often lauded as though it contained a panacea for all human ills. The watchwords of the French Revolution were "Liberty," "Equality," "Fraternity," but never were three grand conceptions so abused and debased. As interpreted by history "Liberty" meant unbridled

---

[1] Luke i. 32. [2] Galatians iii. 28.

license; "Equality" was not the lifting up of the lowly, but the pulling down of all that was high; while "Fraternity" seemed to mean the hatred of demons, reveling in cruelty and blood.

Quite as misleading is the aphorism that all men are created free and equal. The only answer to such a statement is that it is not true. So far as we can see, men are not created "equal" in any sense that properly belongs to the word. Furthermore, perfect freedom and equality are impossible in any scheme of human government so long as human nature remains what it is. But I unhesitatingly affirm that just this ideal state of freedom and equality is the very thing proposed in the kingdom of God. Men who are not free are to be made free by mighty spiritual forces. "Ye shall know the truth, and the truth shall make you free,"[1] is the announcement of the King himself, and is emphasized by the further statement, "If therefore the Son shall make you free, ye shall be free indeed."[2] Then those thus enfranchised are raised by that very process to a position of perfect equality as children of the same Father, subjects of the same kingdom, and heirs of the same heritage on earth and in heaven.

---

[1] John viii. 32. [2] John viii. 36.

It may be well to inquire just here whether history affords any confirmation of the view just advanced. Beyond question the law of the kingdom, as exemplified in the daily life of the primitive Church, accomplished the very result of which I have spoken. National and race barriers that appeared insurmountable were broken down; prejudices that seemed invincible were completely removed; caste and class distinctions, inwoven with the very fibers of society, were obliterated; and without employing a single one of those revolutionary methods that had characterized the history of nations, the divine kingdom effected a revolution that completely changed the moral and social aspects of society. Jew and Greek, barbarian and Scythian, bond and free—all became one in Christ.

An immediate effect of this law of the kingdom touching the equality of all believers is seen in the attitude of the primitive Church toward the question of slavery. At the time when the new kingdom became a living reality, domestic slavery, in some form, was universal. Among the Jews bond-service was an institution as old as the nation, but was surrounded by checks and safeguards that prevented it from degenerating into a system of oppression. Among other nations it was not so. Slavery of the most pronounced type was the rule; and the slave, whether bought with money or taken in battle, had no rights, personal, civil, or social. Such a system among peoples whose religions inculcated no sentiment of humanity, and whose laws imposed no restraint, was sure to result in gross injustice and oppression. In view of this fact, it seems strange that in the Gospels there is no direct allusion to the institution of slavery, or any intimation as to how it should be dealt with in the kingdom of God. Jesus must have known that the problem would confront the Church as soon as it passed the limits of Palestine and began to win converts among the Gentiles; and yet he does not denounce the system as wrong, nor does he enjoin upon his followers the duty of waging relentless war against it. He simply leaves this, as he leaves all other social problems, to be solved by the spirit and genius of the gospel, rather than by any express command.

The wisdom of this policy is seen in the results. Within half a century the Church had solved the problem so far as the kingdom of God was concerned. Without any political agitation or social revolution, the new kingdom brought "liberty to the captives, and the opening of the prison to them that were bound." Indeed, it could not be otherwise. The gospel in its very essence is unalterably opposed to injustice and oppression in any form; and whoever received the gospel, whether he were rich or poor, bond or free, of noble or plebeian blood, at once entered a new kingdom where all were enfranchised and became God's freemen, dowered with the same rights because heirs of the same citizenship. Nay, more: the inward transformation wrought by the gospel not only enfranchised them as members of the same divine commonwealth, it also constituted them members of a common brotherhood in which there could be no distinction on account of race or rank or birth or fortune. They all had become children of a common Father in virtue of a common redemption in Jesus Christ.

This principle of the equality of all believers involved, also, the equality of the sexes, and therefore the emancipation of woman. Probably the highest uninspired conceptions of an ideal human society ever given to the world are to be found in Plato's "Republic" and More's "Utopia"; but the former included human slavery and the abolition of marriage for the higher class as parts of his system, while the latter outlined a state in which class distinctions were by no means abolished. Jesus, on the other hand, taught the sacredness of the individual, and announced the freedom and equality of all men in the kingdom of God. Instead of abolishing marriage or weakening its bond, he elevated and sanctified the relation as the highest, divinest institution possible to the race. For woman, as such, he taught freedom and equality, repudiating the notion, so prevalent at the time in every nation outside of Palestine, that she was merely a chattel, at best a necessary evil, so that the birth of a female child was regarded as a household calamity, as it is to this day in heathen lands. Among the early Christians the great fact of the incarnation, when Jesus was born of a woman, had exalted and glorified once for all the dignity of womanhood, still more of motherhood, and abolished forever the idea of her inferiority. Under the influence of this exalted faith Christians have always and everywhere repudiated polygamy, and held firmly to the doctrine of monogamous marriage which Jesus inculcated. It will be seen, also, that this principle of the equality of the sexes carries with it, as its inevitable corollary, that there can be but one standard of morals, the same for men as for women.

The last, but by no means the least important, principle in the kingdom of God on the earth is that of vicarious sacrifice. Had I been thinking of this only in its relation to Christ's atoning work, it would have been considered first in the series of foundation principles, but my object at present is to call attention to the fact that it not only inheres in the very constitution of the kingdom, but that its practical outcome is the only possible solution of most of our social problems. As commonly understood, even among Christians, self-sacrifice means only some spasmodic efforts to do good, a little self-denial here and there, a little charity, so called, but not enough to infringe upon our own comforts or lessen perceptibly our possessions. But the self-sacrifice which Jesus taught, and exemplified in his life and death, is a very different thing. It meant that "though he was rich, yet for our sakes he became poor, that we through his poverty might become rich";[1] it meant that he bore "our griefs, and carried our sorrows," and that the Lord "laid on him the iniquity of us all";[2] it meant that he "humbled himself, and became obedient unto death, even the death of the cross";[3] and self-sacrifice thus interpreted is of the very essence of his kingdom, and not a mere incidental feature. In a word, it means that he "came not to

---

[1] 2 Corinthians viii. 9.
[2] Isaiah liii. 4-6.
[3] Philippians ii. 8.

be ministered unto, but to minister, and to give his life a ransom for many,"[1] and that all this must be true of the Church if it would be true to its Lord, and fill out his ideal of the kingdom of God.

The principles of the kingdom of God were inevitable factors in shaping its polity. By "polity" in this connection is not meant a code of rules for the government of the Church as an organized community, but rather those principles, scattered through the Gospels, whereby individual Christians are to regulate their conduct toward one another and toward the world at large. It must not be supposed that in establishing the moral standards of the new dispensation there was any violent break with the moral standards of the old. Jesus guards against any such anticipation, warning his disciples that he came not to destroy the law and the prophets, but to fulfill. The Decalogue is just as much a part of the law of Christ's kingdom as is the Sermon on the Mount. He indorsed and reaffirmed its precepts, for these did not belong solely to the law of Moses, but were part of a primal law which had been incorporated with the Jewish system as a summary of moral principles, wide as humanity and lasting as time. The attitude of Je-

---

[1] Matthew xx. 28.

sus toward the Decalogue is clearly seen in his teaching. He affirms the supremacy of God as the only object of religious worship;[1] the duty of honoring father and mother;[2] the necessity of keeping the commandments if we would enter into life, and quotes in this connection no less than five clauses of the Decalogue;[3] and referring in another place to two great precepts, outside of the Ten but breathing the spirit of them all, he affirms that "on these two commandments hangeth the whole law, and the prophets."[4] It is clear, therefore, that Jesus incorporated the Decalogue as the foundation of the polity of his kingdom; but the difference between the old and the new consists in this, that while Jesus taught the same moral precepts as Moses he gave them a new application, and carried them inward from the life to the heart. Moses forbade murder;[5] Christ forbids anger.[6] Moses forbade the unclean act;[7] Christ forbids the unclean thought.[8] Moses said, "Swear not falsely";[9] Christ says, "Swear not at all."[10]

---

[1] Matthew iv. 10. (Compare Deuteronomy vi. 13, 14, and iv. 20, 23.)

[2] Matthew xv. 4. (Compare Exodus xx. 12.)

[3] Matthew xix. 18, 19. [7] Exodus xx. 14.

[4] Matthew xxii. 40. [8] Matthew v. 28.

[5] Exodus xx. 13. [9] Exodus xx. 16.

[6] Matthew v. 22. [10] Matthew v. 34.

The law of revenge said, "An eye for an eye, and a tooth for a tooth;[1] but the law of Christ says, "Resist not evil."[2] In a word, Moses enjoined upon men to keep their *lives* clean; but Christ enjoins upon men to keep their *souls* clean.

The polity of the divine kingdom is seen in what its laws forbid as well as in what they enjoin. It was to be a kingdom in the world but not of it; and its spirit, laws, maxims, policy, methods, were to be the very reverse of those which had obtained in earthly kingdoms. Its organization was to be of the simplest kind. It was to have no visible or human head, but he who was greatest among its citizens was to be servant of all.[3] It was to employ no force,[4] collect no taxes, maintain no army, inflict no punishments, revenge no injuries.[5] Its one sole weapon of discipline was to refuse fellowship with incorrigible offenders.[6] In the kingdom of God personal rights, as commonly understood, were to have no place, save the right of mutual service, rendered with a whole-

---

[1] Exodus xxi. 24.
[2] Matthew v. 39.
[3] Matthew xxiii. 11.
[4] John xviii. 36.
[5] Matthew v. 39.
[6] Matthew xviii. 17; Romans xvi. 7; 1 Corinthians v. 11.

heartedness that seeks for nothing in return, but is content, like the rain or the light, to pour itself out upon all who need.

It is impossible in the compass of this lecture to pass in review all the precepts of the gospel which touch man's social relations; but there is one law of the kingdom which is deserving of special emphasis because it has been suffered to escape, to a large extent, from the working creed of the Church, and also because its restoration is indispensable to the solution of many of our social problems. I refer to the gospel law respecting property, and the way in which its use is to be regulated in the kingdom of God. This doctrine or law held a very prominent place in the faith and practice of the early Christians for nearly three hundred years, and its decline was simultaneous with the incoming of a flood of worldliness which swept the Church so far from her old foundations that she has scarcely got back to them even to this day.

What, then, was the law regarding property or personal possession which came in with the kingdom of God? One thing about it is certain: it was utterly opposed to the laws and customs on the same subject which then prevailed throughout the world, and which still prevail in human governments. The student who makes himself familiar with the language and spirit of the Gospels, and with the daily life of the early Christian Church, will find it hard to resist the conviction that the kingdom of God, in its social aspect, was founded upon the principle of a divine communism, and that the principle was recognized and acted upon for several centuries. From the beginning it was apparent that an era had dawned wherein personal and individual rights receded farther and farther into the background, and community rights became correspondingly prominent. Hitherto individual rights had predominated, and society seemed to be based upon the principle

> "That he should take who has the power,
> And he should keep who can";

but under the beneficent sway of the gospel the right of one became the right of all, the interest of one the interest of all, and, in a very important sense, the possessions of one the possession of all.

It is not to be inferred from this that the gospel sanctions any scheme of confiscation, or makes the possession of property a fault, much less a crime. Neither does it teach that the vicious, the indolent, the thriftless, have a right to share in the earnings of the moral, industrious, and prudent members of the community. Such a scheme would at once put a premium upon vice and idleness. But it does teach that in the kingdom of God the right of private possession was to give place to the responsibilities of stewardship, and that each member of the Christian community should regard himself as holding his possessions in trust for the common good, to be used as the providence of God might indicate, first in providing shelter, food, and raiment for those of his own household, or of kindred whom misfortune might throw upon his bounty, and after that in helping needy brethren and in spreading the kingdom and truth of God in the earth.

I have said that the kingdom of God was founded upon a divine communism, in which the need of one became the care and concern of all; not the Christless communism advocated in some quarters to-day, whose foundation is selfishness and whose outcome will be anarchy; but a communism imbued with the very spirit of Him who " came not to be ministered unto, but to minister," a communism wherein no man said that aught of the things he possessed were his own, but stood ready to distribute to every fellow-citizen as he had need. In all this there was no confiscation of property, no tyrannical overthrow of private rights.

It was a voluntary surrender by those who had become citizens of a heavenly kingdom, and who recognized the fact that the supreme law of the kingdom had abrogated for them both legal codes and social maxims where these conflicted with the law of love. New forms of speech came in to express new conceptions, and even old forms took on new and larger meanings. Those who had entered the kingdom were no longer children of Abraham merely. They had become children of God and stewards of his gifts. They were no longer to be distinguished as Jew and Gentile, Greek and Roman, bond and free; for now all were free, and all were one in Christ Jesus.

The voluntary nature of this property surrender in the primitive Church is evidenced by a specific instance, where the general principle that guided a believer in matters of property comes clearly into view. The account of this matter given in the fourth chapter of the Acts of the Apostles is as follows: "And the multitude of them that believed were of one heart and soul: and not one of them said that aught of the things which he possessed was his own; but they had all things common. And with great power gave the apostles their witness of the resurrection of the Lord Jesus: and great grace was upon them all. For neither was

PRINCIPLES AND POLITY. 71

there among them any that lacked: for as many as were possessors of lands or houses sold them, and brought the prices of the things that were sold, and laid them at the apostles' feet: and distribution was made unto each according as any one had need."[1]

Then follows an account of an attempted deception by Ananias, who sold a possession, but kept back part of the price, and was punished with sudden death from the hand of the Lord. The sin of Ananias was not in bringing a part of the price, but in pretending a part was a whole. This is clearly recognized in the words of Peter: "Ananias, why hath Satan filled thy heart to lie to the Holy Ghost, and to keep back part of the price of the land? Whiles it remained, did it not remain thine own? and after it was sold, was it not in thy power? How is it that thou hast conceived this thing in thy heart? thou hast not lied unto men, but unto God. And Ananias hearing these words fell down and gave up the ghost."[2]

A result so tragic, a punishment so swift and terrible, is very startling, and can be explained only on the supposition that the gospel law respecting property was not a mere incident, but was fundamental

[1] Acts iv. 32-35. [2] Acts v. 3-5.

in the Christian scheme. The definite establishment of the kingdom of God at Pentecost, when the Holy Ghost became sole administrator, introduced a new era, in which believers ceased to be proprietors and became stewards. In discharging the duties of this relation it is of supreme importance that a steward be found faithful,[1] and that transparent truthfulness should characterize all his dealings in the fulfillment of his trust. To lie unto men is bad enough, but to lie to the Holy Ghost hath no forgiveness.

It is worthy of note, however, that this new line of conduct touching the use of property was not due to some express commandment in the Gospels; it was simply the recognition of one aspect of the law of love, and sprang from a divine impulse in the soul. In the faith of the primitive Christians the redemption which had come through Jesus Christ extended not alone to the soul, but to soul and body and property. They had been "bought with a price," had become the willing bond-servants of Jesus Christ, and the idea of withholding anything from him never entered into their thoughts. Hence the impulse which led to the selling of possessions, and using the proceeds

---

[1] Luke xii. 42–46; xvi. 1, 2; 1 Corinthians iv. 2.

for the relief of the needy, was no mere spasm of unregulated enthusiasm; it was the practical outcome of an essential principle of the new kingdom.

At this point the question arises as to how far the practice of the apostolic Church in the use of property is binding upon Christians at the present time. The answer is that the underlying principle is as binding as ever, but that methods may not necessarily be the same. The selling of possessions and casting the proceeds into a common fund was made necessary by the circumstances in which the early Christians were placed. As yet they were few in number, and some were very poor, while others were liable at any moment to be despoiled of their goods through persecution, so that a family that was in comfort to-day might be reduced to absolute beggary to-morrow. It was a wise and necessary arrangement, therefore, which turned all possessions into a common fund out of which the real needs of all might be supplied. But when the kingdom had extended into the regions beyond, and the number of believers was greatly multiplied, the method of one common fund was no longer practicable. It was then that the divine principle of individual stewardship came into prominence—each believer holding in trust that portion of the common estate which Providence had placed in his hands, administering the same for the common good and for the spread of the kingdom of God.

It will be seen that the law of the divine kingdom now under consideration did not abrogate the right of private property, but it changed its uses by changing the tenure on which it was held. To assert, as some do, that the accumulation of private property is robbery, and that its possession is a crime, is not only foolish but wicked. That Christians should prosper in worldly affairs is quite to be expected, for one effect of Christianity, when it is real, is to make men industrious, frugal, economical. Wasting is as foreign to the spirit of the gospel as is hoarding on the one hand or self-indulgence on the other. It is not the accumulation of property that is wrong, but the holding of it for selfish ends and uses. And even where this is done we have no right to call it robbery or crime. All that we are justified in saying is that such a one transfers his allegiance from the kingdom of God to the kingdom of this world, for he practically denies a fundamental law of that kingdom of which he professes to be a subject, and obeys the law of another kingdom which is opposed to that of Christ.

If any one is in doubt whether the law of the kingdom regarding property really demands that complete change of attitude in which no man said that aught of the things he possessed was his own, it may be well to recall some of the sayings of Christ respecting the matter. These sayings can be understood only when we bear in mind that the kingdom of God which Christ came to establish is on the earth and not in the heavens; that what he had in contemplation was an ideal community of men and women here in this world; and as this community in its spirit, policy, customs, and maxims was to be the very reverse of those which obtain in the kingdom of the world, it is plain upon the face of it that to enter Christ's kingdom one must renounce all his past conceptions of things, especially such as are most characteristic of human society as actually existing. Now in the past as in the present nothing was more characteristic of the laws and usages of earthly kingdoms than the recognition of man's absolute right to property which he had acquired; the right to use it as might seem good to him while he lived, and to bequeath it to whom he would when life was closing and he could no longer use it for himself.

I do not here raise the question whether this legal right of absolute proprietorship, as conceded by human governments, is morally right or otherwise; I only say that the principle is not recognized in the laws of the kingdom of God. In that kingdom stewardship and not proprietorship is the universal law, and unless this law is recognized we shall find it hard to explain in a satisfactory way many things which Jesus taught. Let us turn to some of these as recorded in the Gospels, and see if this be so. Take, for example, the case of the rich man who came to Jesus asking what good thing he should do that he might have eternal life. Jesus replied: "Keep the commandments." The young man said: "All these things have I observed: what lack I yet?" Then comes the test: "If thou wouldest be perfect, go, sell that thou hast, and give to the poor, and thou shalt have treasure in heaven: and come, follow me."[1] Apply this to things purely spiritual, make it the condition of entrance into heavenly felicity, and the explanation strikes us at once as forced and unnatural; but regarded as a fundamental law of an ideal community to be established here on earth, in which common rights should take the place of personal rights, and no man would live for self but for the happiness of others, the ex-

---

[1] Matthew xix. 16–22.

planation is simple and consistent. This view is further emphasized by the words that follow: "It is hard for a rich man to enter the kingdom of heaven." And again: "It is easier for a camel to go through a needle's eye, than for a rich man to enter into the kingdom of God."[1] But why should this thing be difficult even to the verge of impossibility? If the reference is only to a spiritual regeneration, and ultimate entrance into the kingdom of glory, the conversion of a rich man is no harder task to the Holy Spirit than is the conversion of a poor man; but if Jesus had in mind a fundamental law of his kingdom in this world, which demanded as a condition of entrance the voluntary surrender of all worldly possessions (not, as has been stated, in the sense of casting all into a common fund, but of holding our possessions in trust and administering the same for the common good), then any one who knows human nature will at once perceive that this is the very thing which no rich man will do save under the power of a dominant conviction that "the thing that is best for all believers is best for him, and that the common good is better than self-aggrandizement."

---

[1] Matthew xix. 23, 24.

Let us now turn to another passage which exemplifies in a yet more striking way the truth that I am trying to impress: "Then Peter began to say unto him, Lo, we have left all, and have followed thee. And Jesus answered and said, Verily I say unto you, There is no man that hath left house, or brethren, or sisters, or father, or mother, or wife, or children, or lands, for my sake, and the gospel's, but he shall receive a hundredfold now in this time, houses, and brethren, and sisters, and mothers, and children, and lands, with persecutions; and in the world to come eternal life."[1]

On the usual lines of interpretation such a statement is utterly unintelligible, but on the supposition that Christ is referring to the believer's position in the kingdom of God here on earth, the meaning is plain. He who relinquished friends and earthly possessions for the gospel's sake entered thereby a kingdom where every fellow-believer was a brother, or sister, or mother, and where he became an equal sharer in all the wealth of the kingdom as far as his just needs required. No matter how much he might have relinquished, he obtained literally "a hundredfold now in this time."

---

[1] Mark x. 28-30.

If the principles enunciated in these observations are sound, and my exegesis can be maintained, two things are clear: First, that the average Church life of the present day is far below the spirit and teachings of Jesus Christ; and, secondly, that the unfeigned acceptance and application of the principles and polity of the kingdom of God by Christians generally would so revolutionize social conditions that it might be declared, not in the language of metaphor but of sober fact: "The kingdom of God is among you."

LECTURE III.

TWO IMPORTANT ISSUES, AND HOW TO MEET THEM.

"Christianity and labor can most naturally enter upon that coöperative pursuit of industrial justice which is the duty of the hour by battling together, first of all, for labor's right to the rest day, the gain of which, to those deprived of it, is greater and easier of attainment than the eight-hour law, and an earnest of all other labor reforms." (Rev. Wilbur F. Crafts, Ph.D., " Practical Christian Sociology," p. 184, Sec. 22.)

"Remember the sabbath day to keep it holy." (Ex. xx. 8.)

"The sabbath was made for man, and not man for the sabbath." (Jesus, Mark ii. 27.)

"If every member would boycott strong drink . . . for five years, and would pledge his word to study the labor question from its different standpoints, we would then have an invincible host arrayed on the side of justice." (T. V. Powderly.)

"Woe unto him that giveth his neighbor drink, . . . and makest him drunken also." (Hab. ii. 15.)

III.
PRELUDE.—THE GOSPEL AS A REMEDY FOR SOCIAL ILLS.

CERTAIN writers and speakers who seem to have fallen into a confirmed habit of exaggerating our social ills, and even of discovering ills that nobody seemed to be conscious of before, are always telling us that some remedy must be found and applied, and they are by no means backward in suggesting remedies. But as regards some of the proposed methods of dealing with real or imaginary ills, it is by no means certain that the remedy may not prove worse than the disease. Where human ills are curable, doubtless some remedy *ought* to be applied; but just here lies the heart of the whole difficulty. Suppose an adequate remedy is found, can men generally be induced to accept it? Experience says, some of them will accept, a great many will not. It is a case where the homely adage, " You can lead a horse to the stream, but you cannot make him drink," is fairly applicable. I am bold to affirm that a remedy for real ills—personal, political, or social—is within reach, a remedy that never fails when honestly applied; but a great many people resolutely oppose its application because it means death to human selfishness. Yet selfishness is the very taproot of all our social ills.

Perhaps the most persistently advertised remedy for existing diseases of the body politic is socialism, but secular democratic socialism is only selfishness in another form. It is the selfishness of the multitude instead of the individual. But will it be any easier to deal with selfishness in the aggregate than to deal with it in detail? If I am living a truly unselfish life, surely it will be easier for me to persuade some other person—friend or neighbor—to live the same kind of life, than to compel a great multitude, to whom I am an utter stranger, to do so. And surely a steady and continuous endeavor, by all humane and unselfish people, to increase the number by inducing others to accept the gospel as a transforming inward power and as a rule of life, will do infinitely more to solve our social problems than an attempt to compel all men by law to live and act *as if* they were humane and unselfish.

If I were to assert that the only really humane and unselfish people in the world are Christian people, it would call forth, in some quarters, a storm of dissent. There are those who would quickly answer: "You are altogether wrong. Not only are many of your Christian people the narrowest and most selfish in the world, but we can point you to many men who repudiate Christianity, whose daily lives show them to be upright, humane, and unselfish—shining examples of the highest virtues, and worthy of imitation by all who aspire to a noble ideal." Now, assuming, for the sake of argument, that what is said of this class—or some of them—is true, it shows clearly that they have been approximating the Christian ideal (whether purposely or not, or by what means, we need not now inquire), and that what these men are said to have repudiated is not Christianity, but some false, distorted image of Christianity which they have seen, or think they have seen, in the average Christian teaching and life of the times.

Waiving altogether for the present the question of the divine origin of Christianity, there are two things which no intelligent skeptic, with any claim to fairness, has ever ventured to dispute—namely, that Jesus of Nazareth is incomparably the noblest, purest, loftiest type of character that has ever appeared among men, and that his gospel embodies principles which, if allowed to govern human affairs, would transform society, and bring about here on earth those ideal conditions foreshadowed in the Christian millennium. It follows, therefore, that the noblest type of manhood possible on earth is that which approximates most closely to Jesus of Nazareth, and that there is no approach toward real purity and goodness in any other direction. It follows, also, that those who would regenerate society, and lift humanity to a higher plane, cannot adopt a better course than to surrender their own inmost nature to the sway of the gospel, and then press that gospel upon the acceptance of other men, with a view to its enthronement as the supreme standard of human conduct in all the affairs of life.

To all this it may be answered: "What you say may be true in a general way, but what we contend for is that men have approximated an ideal character, not only without help from Christian teaching and influences but in repudiation of them, and therefore your Christianity is quite unnecessary either as a moral force for the upbuilding of character, or as a standard of right for the guidance of conduct." But I reply: How do you know that these ideal characters are not a product of the very Christianity which you affect to despise? The devotees of physical science are never weary of telling us that man, as he exists to-day, is the product of three forces, heredity, evolution, and environment; but the very men who repudiate

Christianity are themselves the heirs of a Christian heredity reaching back through many centuries, and have lived, moved, and had their being in an environment that throbs with the influence of Christian truth and Christian institutions. To say that a noble life owes nothing to the only influences that can make it truly noble is a strange and unnatural perversion of the truth.

It has often happened that men, in their desire to avoid a system of ethics which strikes at the root of all self-seeking in Church and State, in business and in social life, have not hesitated to say that the gospel code is too ethereal for this practical age; that ideal conditions of society may be very well as matters of speculation, befitting the rhapsodies of poet or seer, but we need not expect to see them realized this side of heaven. The thought seems to be that Christ's ideal is too lofty for human attainment, and it would be better to concern ourselves with such ameliorations of existing conditions as human legislation and individual philanthropy can supply; that the world has grown too wise to attempt impossibilities, and is willing to content itself with what lies within reach. But such reasoning is based upon a false assumption. It ignores altogether the divine element in the gospel, and the regenerating power of the Holy Spirit. It puts Jesus Christ on a par with the *doctrinaire* reformers who have appeared from time to time, and reduces the kingdom of God to the level of Plato's "Republic" or of More's "Utopia." But Jesus Christ is not like human theorists. He is contemporary with all the ages, and thought and progress never outrun his teaching. From the beginning he foresaw the failure of human systems, and through the ages was preparing something that would supply their place. It was not his purpose to establish an ideal human government, but to create an ideal community, in which government, as commonly understood, would cease to be a necessity; not to attack existing abuses and overturn them by force, but to create conditions in which the abuses could not exist. Unlike all other social reformers, Christ begins at the center instead of the circumference. Instead of changing a man's environment, he touches the hidden springs of his moral nature, producing new affections, new purposes, new desires, and by carrying forward this process from man to man he aims to bring about a state of society in which oppression and wrong become impossible.

Among the many wonderful sayings of Christ there is one which deserves more careful consideration than it has commonly received: "If ye abide in me, and my words abide in you, ask whatsoever ye will, and it shall be done unto you."[1] But how can we be said to abide in Christ if we keep not his word? or how can his words be said to abide in us if we refuse to accept them in their obvious meaning, or to put them in practice in our lives? There would appear to be only one way of escaping from the dilemma, and that is to affirm, as some do, that the words of Christ should not be interpreted literally; that they are to be understood in a general sense and usually with a spiritual meaning—not in such a way as to conflict with common sense and render the commands themselves impracticable. But has any one a right to say that the words of Jesus, even when taken literally, are impracticable? One thing is certain, if they were taken in their plain obvious sense and obeyed, society would be quickly transformed, and heaven would begin on earth. And no man has the right to say that Christ's commands are impracticable until he has honestly tried to obey them. Assuredly the practice of explaining away the words of Jesus—of giving them some other meaning than the obvious one—has not been a success. It has resulted only in robbing the Church

---

[1] John xv. 7.

of her strength and making the promises of God of none effect.

There is only one way of knowing the truth, and that is by obeying it. Very many have fallen into the error of supposing that truth is reached by controversy or by criticism, and have wearied themselves and wearied the world by suggesting innumerable possible meanings of the words of Scripture, none of which they have thought it necessary to put in practice. The result is that they have not only "darkened counsel by words without knowledge," but have given a bent to their own moral nature which makes the apprehension of truth a difficult if not an impossible thing. To know the truth and then to dispute about it, or to evade instead of doing it, is morally disastrous in the highest degree. It both darkens the perceptive powers and blunts the moral sense. The only safe course, when once truth is known, is to let it pass into immediate action. Then shall we know more, for there is nothing so illuminating as obedience. In all this I am propounding no new doctrine. I am only pleading for a practical acceptance of what, as Christians, we already profess to believe. I only ask that Christ's words be taken, just as they stand, as words to be obeyed. No middle course is possible. We must either accept the truth as it is and practice it, or we must utterly repudiate it as a rule of life.

The Church and society are being brought face to face, as never before, with the words of Jesus Christ. So clearly is this perceived that some have boldly challenged the authority of Christ's commands, where they conflict with their own judgment of what is right and proper. Thus a Unitarian divine of the present day,[1] speaking of certain words of Jesus, asks: "What shall we say of these? Are we bound by them in defiance of our common sense and our enlightened Christian judgment? No! we must conclude that these are the mere details, incidental and unessential; partly of local and temporary expediency, and partly the enthusiastic excesses of a reformer; the extravagances of a God-intoxicated idealist. And besides, Jesus was a poet. Many of his sayings were poetical. Whole discourses fall into the form of verse. The beautiful, the matchless *spirit* of Jesus' life will ever remain an inspiration to the highest living; his actual words and acts must not, of course, be allowed to weigh against our practical common sense."

---

[1] Rev. Dr. Brooke Herford, quoted by Rev. William Bayard Hale in "The New Obedience," page 29.

If such views are to be accepted, then the standard of duty and holy living is no longer the words of the great Revealer of God, but only the "practical common sense" whereby every man becomes a law unto himself. But that Christ intended his words to be obeyed in their plain obvious meaning is clear from his own teaching. At the close of that wonderful discourse which we call the Sermon on the Mount, he sums up the difference between doing and merely knowing the things he has commanded, likening the first to a wise man who built his house upon a rock, and the other to a foolish man who built his house upon the sand.[1] "These sayings of mine," as the Master calls them, are not, as the Unitarian divine would have us believe, "mere details, incidental and unessential"; they are the very foundation without which we cannot build with safety or success. In former times the only dispute was in regard to the meaning of the words themselves, and men tried to evade their force by the plea that they were to be understood in some vague spiritual sense; but to-day it is felt that if accepted at all the words must be taken as they are, that the only way of escape is to deny their authority.

---

[1] Matthew vii. 24–27.

There is a very widespread notion that the gospel has to do only with matters purely spiritual; that the kingdom of which it speaks is not here but in the heavens, and that it has nothing to say about the shaping of human conduct in this life. If any attempt is made to apply New Testament principles to everyday life, or to special phases of moral conduct, such as Sabbath observance, the liquor traffic, social vice, the purification of politics, or the like, there are persons not a few who resent such application and say to Christian ministers: "Preach the gospel; you have no right to interfere with other things in the pulpit." It need not surprise us if such persons have the idea that there is nothing in the laws of the kingdom of God respecting man's social relations in this world, especially anything that touches the question of property. But a careful reading of the Gospels ought to dispel this illusion. There is no social or even political relation common to man which the gospel does not touch and for which it does not provide. In the nature of the case this must be so. The kingdom of God is first and chiefly in this world, and to establish a kingdom in a world where questions of social relations, of political obligations, of property rights and responsibilities, must continually arise, and yet to have no word as to how these various questions should be met and answered, would lead to the conclusion that the Founder of the kingdom must be lacking in ordinary common sagacity, let alone in wisdom of a higher kind.

LECTURE III.—TWO IMPORTANT ISSUES, AND HOW TO MEET THEM.

A QUESTION of vital importance to the physical, social, and moral well-being of the whole people is the maintenance of the Lord's day as a time of rest for all, and an opportunity for religious worship for such as are willing so to spend it. It would be a great mistake to regard this as a purely religious question. That aspect has an interest for religious people, and properly so; but in its moral and social aspects it has, or should have, an interest for everybody, whether they are religious or not. That man's physical well-being, to go no farther, demands frequently recurring periods of complete cessation from toil scarcely needs to be affirmed, because the fact is universally recognized and admitted. Such periods of rest are demanded as emphatically by the law of nature as by the law of Moses. It is true that the first appearance of the Sabbath as a positive law, with specific duties and weighty sanctions, is in the Hebrew code; but the reason assigned for its institution seems to point back to a primal law, while the emphatic statement of Christ that "the Sabbath was made for man" indicates as plainly as words can do its vast importance as regards human welfare. An institution designed by divine wisdom and goodness expressly for man's benefit should hold no secondary place in any scheme of society or government.

Those who have watched the trend of affairs must be aware that very serious inroads have been made upon Sabbath rest and quiet within the past four or five decades. Society, in regard to this question, is upon a down grade, and the end is not yet. We have got so far away from the starting point of even a generation ago that the battle of the future, for many a day to come, will be an endeavor to recover lost ground as well as to defend remaining outposts. A vast amount of work is now done on the Lord's day that was not done on that day thirty or forty years ago, and forms of Sabbath amusement and dissipation are common now that public opinion formerly tabooed. The operating of railways for both freight and passenger traffic—of itself an enormous industry—entails a vast amount of Sunday labor, the greater part of it entirely unnecessary. In like manner the carrying and distribution of mails, the running of a certain class of factories, the publishing of Sunday newspapers, telephone and telegraphic communication, running Sunday street cars, Sunday excursions by train or steamer, open saloons, public games, and a hundred things besides, have all become common within a generation, involving the compulsory labor of tens of thousands of working people, for no better reason than that they may minister to the greed of some and to the selfish pleasure of others. I am not now raising the question whether Sunday work or Sunday recreations are morally right or wrong; that is a point to be considered by itself. At present I am only calling attention to the facts in their relation to the physical and social well-being of our fellow-men.

The right of every man to one day in seven for rest (I do not now say religion) is universal and absolute. It is God's gift to his creatures, and should not be lightly tampered with. It is sanctioned by the law of God, and it inheres in the very nature of man. Experience has demonstrated that God's division of time subserves the purpose of human well-being better than any artificial division that man can make. Nothing answers so well as six days for labor and recreation, with every seventh day for rest and worship. France tried the experiment of abolishing the Christian Sabbath and substituting a tenth-day interval; but they soon discovered that the change would not answer, and so went back to the seventh day again. But in the meantime the fetters of compulsory Sunday labor had been fastened upon French workmen, just as they are being fastened upon American workmen to-day, and they toil on in the dreary round of drudgery, doing seven days' work for six days' pay. A similar thing has happened in Chicago. There wage-earners were induced by certain firms to work on Sunday by the promise of seven days' pay, but when the plan had been fairly inaugurated excuses were quickly found for reducing the pay to its former figure, but without any corresponding reduction of the hours of work. It has been scientifically demonstrated that persons engaged in ordinary labor expend their store of energy in a certain ratio, and that a twenty-four hours' rest, each seventh day, is necessary to restore it to its former value, and no other method has been discovered that will answer equally well.

Attempts to secularize the Christian Sabbath, either by multiplying forms of unnecessary labor or by employing the sacred hours for purposes of amusement or dissipation, are based, for the most part, upon selfish considerations. A good deal of random talk has been indulged in about a "Puritan Sunday" and "Connecticut blue laws," but all this is quite irrelevant. In Sunday observance as we have it on this continent there is little enough, in all conscience, resembling a Puritan Sunday; and in our Sunday laws there is nothing which bears the most distant resemblance to the famous, if somewhat mythical, blue laws. While admitting that what is called a Puritan Sunday may not represent the highest ideal of the Lord's day, yet if we have regard to its influence upon the moral, social, and family life of the people, a Puritan Sunday is much to be preferred to a Parisian or a Chicago Sunday. And if the only alternative were that just presented, even then the clean, if somewhat austere, Sabbath bequeathed by the men of the *Mayflower* should appeal more strongly to the patriotism and moral sense of the American people than the befouled and corrupted Sabbath which foreign ignorance and atheism and native greed are seeking to impose upon society. Equally irrelevant is the plea that Sabbath laws infringe the liberties of the citizen. Every law upon the statute book restricts the liberty of the individual citizen in some direction for the general good, Sunday laws no more than any other. It is a safe maxim that "right wrongs no man," and while contending for our own rights we must take care that we do not deprive other people of theirs. The right of every man to his rest day should be indefensible, and only selfishness or greed would seek to deprive him of it.

At this point I raise a question which may have an appearance of invidiousness, though not so intended—namely, Who are the persons or classes who desire to secularize the Lord's day? The question is easily answered. First, those whose object, to state the case with absolute frankness, is to make money out of Sunday labor, and against this considerations of public morality or the rights of workingmen seem to have no weight. Second, the irreligious; the class (not very large, I hope) who would turn God's rest day into a day of amusement, dissipation, and revelry; the class who neither fear God nor regard man; the class to whom all law is an unwelcome restraint, and who are shrewd enough to see that if God's law is ignored human laws that are good for anything will quickly disappear or be entirely disregarded. Third, a considerable portion of those who, for want of a better word, I call the non-religious class. Many of these may be upright citizens, and quite sincere; but, having no deep religious convictions, they have no adequate idea of the value of religious institutions, and hence have no conscientious scruples about turning to secular uses a day which God has made sacred to rest and religion. And yet not a few of this very class, who do not value the Sabbath from religious considerations, see its great value from a social and economic point of view, and for that reason would preserve it as a day of rest.

The class that will suffer more than any other from attacks upon the Sabbath is the working class. They are agitating in many places for an eight-hour working day, and to that I offer no objection; but just at present it would be more to the purpose if they would agitate for the protection of the rest day which many of them still have, but which is in danger of being lost by the encroachments of Mammon on the one hand and of pleasure-seekers on the other. It is gratifying to know that workingmen are speaking out on this question with no uncertain voice through their trade and labor councils; and although their appeal is based upon other than religious considerations, they should have the cordial support of all religious people in the endeavor to defend the day of rest from further encroachments. If it is held that in some places—large cities, for example—some must work on the Lord's day to protect property, to supply light and water, to prepare food, to wait upon the sick or the like, it is manifestly the duty of every good citizen, much more of every Christian, to keep these necessary forms of labor within the narrowest possible limits, rather than to compel men to work where no real necessity exists for so doing. It must be confessed that some Christians have not been consistent in this matter. By patronizing Sunday papers, Sunday street cars, Sunday travel, and by holding their peace when the day is increasingly desecrated by various forms of public amusement, they have lent their influence, as far as it goes, to the complete secularization of the Lord's day, and in doing so have helped to bind upon the shoulders of labor a burden which it ought not to bear.

A great many Christians need to be reminded that the authority of the fourth commandment is not a thing of the past. The Decalogue, as already pointed out, does not belong to the same class of laws as do other parts of the Levitical code, although it is the root of them all. It is a summary of great moral principles, wide as humanity and lasting as time, and there is no hint in the Scriptures that any part of it has ever been repealed or has become obsolete. We are not at liberty to tamper with the divine code by eliminating such portions as may interfere with our selfish aims. The same reasoning which discards the fourth commandment, as no longer binding, applies with equal force to the second, or sixth, or eighth, which forbid image worship, murder, and stealing, unless it can be distinctly shown that in the teaching of Jesus Christ the fourth commandment was excepted, while others were not. The argument, so often heard, that if the fourth commandment remains it must be observed only on the seventh day of the week, and in all the minutiæ of the letter, has no real weight. Revelation has ever been progressive, and the divine purpose in it all has been a steady advance from that which is natural to that which is spiritual. The commandments, as expounded by Jesus Christ, received a new and wider application, as I have elsewhere attempted to show,[1] and hence a Jewish fulfillment of the fourth commandment would not measure up to the Christian ideal, for "except" our "righteousness" —in this as well as in other matters—" shall exceed the righteousness of the scribes and Pharisees," we " shall in no case enter into the kingdom of heaven."[2] The change from the seventh day

---

[1] Lecture II., p. 35. [2] Matthew v. 20.

of the week to the first is justified alike by the circumstances of the case and by the practice of the Church in apostolic times. It maintained the fundamental principle of one day in seven devoted to rest and worship, thus fulfilling the spirit of the commandment. And as the Jewish Sabbath commemorated the finished work of creation when God rested from his labors, the Christian Lord's day commemorates something greater far, even the finished work of redemption when Christ arose from the dead. Paul reminds us that "without any dispute the less is blessed of the better."[1] Now, by so much as the spirit is better than the letter, and the antitype is better than the type, the Christian Lord's day is better than the Jewish Sabbath; hence the latter is not degraded or abrogated by a transference from the seventh day of the week to the first, but is ennobled thereby and consecrated to still higher aims and uses.

Now, when we consider the important place which the day of rest occupies in the divine scheme of government, its intimate connection with both morals and religion, its beneficial and far-reaching influence upon human character in

---

[1] Hebrews vii. 7.

everything that relates to moral development and to family and social life, the attitude of Christian people toward this beneficent institution, and toward all attempts to invade its sacredness, should not be difficult to define. That they are under very weighty obligations to hallow God's day of rest should need no proof, for it is only by hallowing it that its benefits can be realized. As Christians we have no right to import into our Sabbath engagements anything that tends to violate its sanctity or to frustrate the purpose for which it was given. If this principle is admitted, it will rule out not a few things in which some who are called Christians now indulge. It will rule out the Sunday newspaper, which is not only demoralizing in itself but lays upon many an unnecessary burden of work on the Lord's day. It will rule out Sunday travel, because it compels others to work for our convenience; and Sunday excursions for the same reason, and also because they do not tend to recuperate powers that have been taxed by labor, but leave the participant less fit for resuming life's duties than before. It will rule out Sunday amusements, because they are morally dissipating, and open the door for many other evils. It will put an end to Sunday visiting, because, while it may be pleasant recreation to us, it may interfere with our neighbor's plans for rest and devotion. Should some one object and say that this is drawing the checkrein too tightly, it may be sufficient answer to say that every one of the practices just enumerated, with others that might be mentioned, have a direct tendency to pull down instead of building up the kingdom of God among men, and therefore should be steadily resisted by every loyal citizen of the heavenly kingdom.

There is one other question which, even in this brief survey, must not be overlooked: To what extent are we justified in seeking the aid of the civil power to protect the Sabbath? The answer is not difficult. With the Sabbath as a purely religious institution the civil power has nothing to do; but with the Sabbath as a rest day, intimately connected with man's physical and social well-being, it has much to do. The chief function of government, as at present constituted, is to protect the life, liberty, and property of every citizen, and among the citizen's most precious liberties is the liberty to enjoy his weekly rest day, unmolested by the selfishness or greed of others. How, then, are Christians to meet the issue forced upon them by encroachments upon the sanctity of the Lord's day? 1. By abstaining themselves from all unnecessary labor, and devoting the day to rest and worship. 2. By refusing Christian fellowship with those who turn it into a day of money-getting, or of selfish worldly pleasure. 3. By diligently instructing the people, in the Church and out of it, as to the blessings and advantages of keeping God's law. 4. By earnest appeals to workingmen, who more than any other class are interested in this matter, to defend their rights and preserve their liberties. 5. By such legislation as will protect all citizens alike from the selfishness of those who would compel any of them to toil seven days in the week.

Another issue of the gravest kind is presented in the drinking usages of society and the legalized traffic in strong drink. In regard to drinking usages it cannot be said that "the former times were better than these." In this respect there has been a vast change for the better in the last hundred years. Not only is drunkenness branded as disgraceful, but social drinking, at one time universal, is now limited to certain sections of society, and some of these by no means the most reputable. Wine has been banished from ten thousand tables where once it was common. Abstinence, which was ridiculed a hundred years ago as unmanly weakness, is now honored as a social virtue, and public opinion in some countries is turning strongly in the direction of the entire prohibition of the traffic. The scientific aspect of the question is taught in the public schools of the United States and Canada, and a whole generation is being trained up with a knowledge of the nature and injurious effects of alcohol far beyond what was known by the average professional man half a century ago. The Churches are almost a unit in regard to the evils of the traffic, and some of them have spoken out again and again with no uncertain sound. In many of the denominations on this continent, including the larger and more influential, social drinking is virtually unknown, and they have declared through their representative assemblies, in the most emphatic way, that the liquor traffic cannot be licensed without sin. All this shows how many are the milestones that society has passed on its onward march from universal drinking customs toward universal abstinence and the legal prohibition of the traffic.

At the same time it would be very unwise to conclude that the power of the liquor traffic is wholly broken, or that drinking customs have entirely ceased. The battle that seemed to be almost won in one generation has to be fought over again in the next, and the foe dislodged from one stronghold seeks refuge in another. The drink traffic as a social custom is weaker than of yore; as a political power it is vastly stronger, and herein lies the chief danger of the future. One mistake of the past has been in allowing this dangerous foe to society to intrench itself behind legislation, and to surround itself with strong legal ramparts. Not content with this, it has laid its hands upon the very sources of political power, so that from the primary caucus to the national convention its presence and power are felt. To dislodge an enemy so intrenched will be no easy task, and it never will be done so long as loyalty to a political party takes precedence of loyalty to Christ and his kingdom. While intemperance as a moral evil can be dealt with only by moral and spiritual forces, it is not going too far to say that the liquor traffic is virtually an organized conspiracy against the sanctity of the home and the freedom of the State that can be met and conquered only at the ballot box. But this is not likely to be done until citizens in general, and Christian citizens in particular, are so convinced of the magnitude of the evil as to make its removal their foremost duty.

The liquor traffic, beyond all dispute, is the most prodigal waster of both private and national resources, and therefore is a deadly foe to the material interests of society. The manufacture involves an enormous waste of food products which are sorely needed to feed the hungry. The sale and consumption inflicts further waste by taking from society the products of labor while giving nothing of value in return. The economic results of the traffic are disastrous, but the moral and social results are infinitely worse. It works havoc in the home, blighting character, poisoning domestic happiness, reducing children to beggary, and entailing hereditary disease. It is responsible, directly or indirectly, for not less than two-thirds— probably much more—of the pauperism and crime which entail such heavy financial burdens upon society. To sum up the indictment, the liquor traffic wastes resources, degrades character, wrecks the home, corrupts politics, fosters immorality and crime, fills jails, poorhouses, and asylums, lays upon society a large share of its financial burdens, draws from productive labor enormous revenues, but renders no real service to society in return. In a word, the liquor traffic is a social parasite, costly but useless, whose utter destruction would inflict no real loss upon the State.

The liquor traffic is an unrelenting foe to the kingdom of God—one of the most dangerous and deadly of them all. Worse than war or pestilence, it slays not only the bodies, but also the souls of men. The strongest intellects have been paralyzed by its potent wizardry, and the noblest Christian characters have been debauched by the spell of its unholy enchantments. It has robbed the pulpit of its brightest ornaments, and bench and bar have been darkened by the shadow of its dread eclipse. It benumbs the conscience while it inflames the passions, and hurls perverted reason from its throne. It steels the heart to the claims of affection, and poisons the springs of happiness at the fountain head. Like the Circean enchantress, it changes men into swine by means of a magic drink, and upon such degenerate natures argument and appeal have no effect. Among the barbarous tribes of Africa it constitutes a barrier to the spread of the gospel more difficult to overcome than the darkest heathenism, while the intemperance it induces among men from Christian lands is the standing reproach against Christianity among the non-Christian tribes and nations of the world.

With such a foe the kingdom of God can hold no parley and make no compromise. Her attitude toward the liquor traffic and the drinking customs of society must be one of resolute and undisguised antagonism. This modern Goliath has defied the armies of the living God, and for them to sound a retreat, or even ask for a parley, would be arrant cowardice, as well as disloyalty to their King and Lord. The Church must keep steadily before it, as the ultimate goal, the entire extinction of the traffic, and in the meantime must see to it that whoever may afford aid and comfort to this foe of society it shall find no refuge within the limits of the kingdom of God. But all this must be done on grounds and by methods that are in harmony with New Testament ethics and will commend themselves to thoughtful and impartial men. It is easy, and not uncommon, for advocates of total abstinence and prohibition to overdo things by extravagant statements and random assertions that become boomerangs, rebounding with telling effect upon the hand that flung them. All this is quite unnecessary. A strong and unanswerable impeachment of the liquor traffic can be formulated that is well within the lines of truth. Ample reasons to justify total abstinence can be found without the very questionable assertions that the use of wine is always and everywhere condemned in the Scriptures, or that the wine which Jesus used was not fermented. And solid arguments for the legal proscription of the traffic can be constructed without making statements that cannot be verified, or manipulating statistics to suit our own views.

The effect of an organized liquor traffic upon politics, upon trade and commerce, upon the moral, social, and family life of the people, as well as upon individual character, are attracting more and more the attention not only of philanthropists and social reformers, but also of statesmen, scientists, and men of affairs. The issues presented are so grave that they cannot be dealt with by existing machinery, but require a method of treatment peculiarly their own. Other forms of industrial activity can be left to develop on their own lines and to any extent, and it is generally admitted that the best results follow when trade is free from all restrictions within the limits that properly belong to it. But the liquor traffic is the one great exception. It cannot be intrusted with freedom of development. It must be regulated, controlled, repressed, hedged around with restrictions like a dangerous pitfall, lest the helpless or the unwary should fall therein. All this stamps the traffic as a dangerous menace to society—something to be watched and guarded against, or, in the opinion of many, exterminated altogether. That society would gain enormously in wealth, in social comfort and domestic happiness by the destruction of the traffic, no unprejudiced man who is familiar with the facts can doubt; but as yet there has not been, in most places, that consensus of opinion as to methods which admits of effective political action, and the traffic still continues its deadly work.

It is conceded on all sides that the liquor traffic cannot be let alone, for the simple reason that it will not let society alone. It must be dealt with in some way, and the authority to deal with it is based upon the indefeasible right of society to protect itself against anything which is a menace to its prosperity or happiness. A great many experiments have been tried, none of which have been entirely successful; but the time and effort have not been altogether wasted. Something has been gained, if only in a negative way, by learning what methods may as well be dropped because they do not meet the case, and what modifications of other methods may lead to ultimate success. Whatever may be said of political or semi-political methods, nothing has yet occurred which discounts the value of moral and spiritual forces in combating the drinking customs of society, although it may be feared that in prosecuting so vigorously our appeal unto Cæsar the moral and spiritual agencies have fallen into abeyance. The marked change for the better in the habits of society regarding the use of strong drink has been brought about almost exclusively by moral suasion, backed by Christian example, and points to the wisdom of steady and continuous effort along similar lines. Even with prohibition as the result to be aimed at, moral forces, rather than political, must lead the van, for wise and beneficent laws are the effect of enlightened public opinion, not its cause; and in a land where the principles of democratic self-government obtain, the best laws would be useless unless sustained by a healthy public sentiment.

The principal methods hitherto tried of dealing with the liquor traffic may be classed under the following heads: 1. Free trade in strong drink. This was virtually tried in Norway, where at one period any one who chose might have a private still, and manufacture brandy to any extent. The results were so disastrous that the plan had to be abandoned. 2. Moral suasion, aiming at universal total abstinence, and the consequent discontinuance of the traffic. 3. Regulation, which involves the licensing system, with police supervision. 4. Direct State control. This has assumed two forms, one of which was tried for a brief period in South Carolina, and the other is now in operation in Scandinavia. 5. Local option, or giving to municipalities the right to prohibit the sale of strong drink within their own borders. 6. Entire prohibition by the State of the manufacture, importation, and sale of intoxicating liquors except for manufacturing, medicinal, and scientific purposes. Each of these methods, except the first, has strenuous advocates, while most of them are by others strongly opposed. It is necessary, therefore, that the whole liquor problem should still be carefully studied from every point of view, so that society may be led to adopt those methods which have proved to be most efficient in repressing what is admitted on all hands to be a social evil of the first magnitude.

Of the policy of free trade in strong drink it is not necessary to speak, as scarcely any one proposes that. It was advocated some years ago by the late Henry George, of New York, on the ground that all restriction is an error, because it forms a rum power, and this rum power was, in his estimation, the dangerous thing. But he argues on the same ground that there should be no customs duties, and no taxes except on land, because they concentrate business in the hands of a few who become a corrupt and corrupting power. Of moral suasion, and its permanent place in the temperance reform, something more will be said farther on; meanwhile a little space may be given to the consideration of various forms of regulation or control. The first of these is the present license system, which goes upon the assumption that as the manufacture and sale of intoxicants cannot be prevented, it ought to be regulated and controlled. But this is not all. It goes upon the further assumption that it is right to license a prolific cause of immorality, pauperism, and crime, and to derive a revenue from the vices of the people. This cannot be admitted. The principle is morally wrong, and "that which is morally wrong cannot be politically right." Long experience has proved that the licensing system, as we have it, is vicious in principle and powerless as a remedy, and no plea of necessity or expediency can possibly justify it. Whatever may be the attitude of the mere politician to this question, it is clear that men who are citizens of the kingdom of God, and are governed by the ethics of the New Testament, can give no countenance to a system that is morally wrong in principle and morally disastrous in results. If we must have a license system, as some assert, let it be one which derives no public revenue from the debasing business, and which holds those who are engaged in it strictly responsible for any injury to health, life, or property which can be proved to be the direct result of it.

Direct State control, as already stated, has assumed two forms, the one in South Carolina and the other in Norway. The South Carolina law was passed in 1892, and although it was subsequently declared unconstitutional by the supreme court of the state, it is referred to as an interesting experiment toward solving the problem of the liquor traffic. According to this law private liquor-selling is abolished, and a system of state dispensaries substituted. There is a state board of control, composed of the governor, comptroller-general, and attorney-general; a state commissioner, who is an abstainer, and a county board of control composed of three members, also abstainers. Dispensaries are opened at the request of a majority of freehold voters. The liquors are purchased by the state commissioner (preference being given to manufacturers doing business in the state), analyzed by the state chemist, put up in quantities varying from half a pint to five gallons, shipped to the dispensaries, and sold at a profit not exceeding fifty per cent.[1] Several advantages are claimed on behalf of this system: 1. Personal profit being eliminated, all incentive to increase sales is removed. 2. Treating is stopped, as the bottles are not opened on the premises. 3. Sales are made only in the daytime. 4. The absence of ice, su-

---

[1] R. E. L. Gould, in *Forum*, November, 1894, page 343.

gar, lemons, etc., and the prohibition of sale by the single drink, remove inducements which have led many astray. 5. Sales are for cash only, and there is no " chalking up " for daily drinks against the workman's pay day. 6. Most important of all, if true, the local whisky rings, which have always controlled municipal elections, have been torn up root and branch.[1] On the other hand, it may be alleged that the object of the law was to raise revenue rather than to decrease drinking, and that local whisky rings may be replaced by a state politico-liquor machine. But even this might be borne in view of the advantages resulting from selling only in the daytime, the abolition of treating, and the breaking up of gambling dens and other immoral adjuncts of the saloon.[2]

The Norwegian system and the South Carolina law are alike in one respect: they both eliminate private profit from the sale of strong drink. In some other respects the methods are widely different. In South Carolina the traffic becomes a state monopoly, all the profits going into the public exchequer. This makes liquor-selling a part of the machinery of the government, and almost guarantees the permanency of the traffic. On the

---

[1] Governor Tillman's Message, 1894.
[2] R. E. L. Gould, in *Forum*, November, 1894, page 344.

Norwegian plan the municipality benefits by the profits, it is true, which is the weak point in the system, but the companies by whom the traffic is carried on receive no profits beyond the current interest on the small capital invested, the object being to control and restrict the traffic until such time as licensing may be altogether abolished. It is claimed that, as a result of this policy, a majority of the inhabitants of the Scandinavian peninsula are already under a no-license or local option *régime*, while the membership in total abstinence societies has increased from a mere handful to over three hundred thousand. Moreover, in Norway every vestige of political influence has been eliminated from the traffic. As a further proof of the advantages of the system, it is affirmed by those who are in a position to know the facts: 1. That no single community in Scandinavia that has tried the plan has afterwards abandoned it. 2. That liquor-selling has been practically abolished throughout the country districts and smaller communities in Norway and Sweden. 3. That the most pronounced temperance men are not seeking to abolish the system, but admit that if liquor is to be sold at all the Norway plan of control is the best that has yet been tried. 4. That since the plan was fully adopted the consumption of spirits in Sweden has declined from 14.2 to 6.8 quarts per annum for each inhabitant, and in Norway from 6.8 to 3.3 quarts. It has to be admitted, however, that while the consumption of ardent spirits has greatly declined, the consumption of beer has largely increased. But as there are no restrictions on the sale of beer, it only shows that the element of private gain is a potent factor in developing the traffic.

Local option is prohibition on a small scale. It has its advocates, and there may be cases where it would result in certain benefits; but as a method of dealing with the evils of the traffic it is altogether inadequate, and should be accepted, if at all, only under protest and as a temporary expedient. Among other defects, it puts the community in the embarrassing position of trying to enforce prohibition under conditions that permit only the minimum of good results. Local option in a township, or even a county, can be of little use while a city or large town on its borders is under license; and in any case it tends to develop the traffic in adjoining municipalities. This was the result in Michigan, where the ratio of licenses to population in places not under local option increased, during the last census period, eight per cent.

From a political and especially a social point of

view, the only rational and effective method of dealing with the traffic is prohibition, pure and simple, although that may require an educational process by less stringent measures. Either the liquor traffic is a legitimate and useful branch of trade, the general effect of which is beneficial to the community, or it is not. If it is legitimate and beneficial, there is no reason why it should be restricted, or why a man should pay a license fee, high or low, for permission to engage in it. The fact is everybody knows, though everybody will not say as much, that the traffic is injurious and dangerous, and that in the interests of society it must be controlled and its ravages restricted within the narrowest possible limits. To accomplish this the license system has been devised, which proceeds virtually on the monstrous assumption that, although the traffic is most injurious, the license fee which the liquor-seller pays is a sufficient compensation for the injury which his trade inflicts upon the community. Such a policy is utterly indefensible save on the ground of the alleged fact that public opinion will not, as yet, indorse a strictly prohibitory *régime.*

Among the more obvious causes that hinder the complete suppression of the liquor traffic may be reckoned the following: 1. A superficial sense of the evils of the traffic, and of the drinking customs of society. This is where the forces of moral suasion should come into play, and all Christian men and women should bestir themselves to create a more vigorous public sentiment on the question. 2. The appetite for stimulants, which grows with the rush and hurry of this feverish age. 3. The greed of gain. This is one of the strong factors with which we have to reckon, and its power can be broken only by eliminating the element of gain alike from the persons who carry on the business and from the communities where it is carried on. 4. Partisan politics, the worst hindrance of all. This, of a truth, is the Goliath that champions the Philistine host and defies the armies of the living God; the insidious power that divides the Church against itself and makes united effort in moral reforms practically impossible. A divided Christian vote is the rampart behind which the liquor traffic lies intrenched, and from that position it cannot be dislodged till Christian citizens learn to put principle before party, and to esteem the triumph of any political organization as of infinitely less moment than the triumph of the kingdom of God.

The mistake of thousands of professing Christians lies in assuming that a double allegiance is possible: that on the religious side they can be devoted servants of God, while on the business and political side they are worldly in policy, partisan in spirit, and selfish in object and aim. The thing is impossible. The kingdom of the world is one thing, the kingdom of God is another, and no man can be a citizen of both at the same time. Under ordinary circumstances this may not be realized, but when great moral issues are to the front then we come to the parting of the ways where each man must decide for himself into which scale his influence shall be cast, and whether loyalty to Christ or political partisanship shall dominate his course of action. In the temperance problem such an issue is before us. The Christian vote, if united and resolute, could outlaw the saloon to-morrow, and sweep away its awful train of attendant miseries, and the only thing that divides the vote is our wretched partisan politics. If there be one man claiming citizenship in the heavenly kingdom who hesitates, under these circumstances, as to what course he should take, let him answer it to his conscience and his God.

LECTURE IV.

THE PROBLEM OF POVERTY.

"The destruction of the poor is their poverty." (Prov. x. 15.)

"For the poor shall never cease out of the land: therefore I command thee, saying, Thou shalt surely open thine hand unto thy brother, to thy needy, and to thy poor, in thy land." (Deut. xv. 11.)

"When the ear heard me, then it blessed me; and when the eye saw me, it gave witness to me: because I delivered the poor that cried, and the fatherless, and him that had none to help him." (Job xxix. 11, 12.)

"By striving to educate, intellectually, morally, sanitarily, the poor, we have made them half conscious of many needs they never recognized before. They were once naked and not ashamed, but we have taught them better. We have raised the standard of the requirements of a decent human life, but we have not increased to a corresponding degree their power to attain them." (John A. Hobson, M.A., "Problems of Poverty," p. 28.)

"For a true human life the essential external requisites are adequate food, shelter, leisure, and provision for incapacity and old age. . . . It is stated on good authority that only one-third of our population are able to live in decent comfort. It is certain that large numbers have no reserve of means, and are unable to make provision for incapacity or old age." (Bishop of Durham, "The Incarnation and Human Duties.")

"Do we not hear them saying it right out with a bluntness that should make us wince: 'Give us no more of your promissory notes; we will cash no more of your bills on a future heaven. Instead of tracts, give us loaves. Instead of a house not made with hands, give us clean and wholesome dwellings. Instead of rest hereafter, give us leisure here to think about it.'" (A. Scott Matheson, "The Church and Social Problems," p. 13.)

IV.

*PRELUDE.—INEQUALITY OF WEALTH AND IN-
EQUALITY OF OPPORTUNITY.*

THE pet grievance with many who speak or write on sociological topics is the unequal distribution of wealth. "The rich growing richer, and the poor growing poorer," is the postulate upon which the changes are rung with monotonous persistency, and the "injustice" of such a condition is affirmed with a great deal of needlessly vehement rhetoric. Now "justice" is a grand word, and it stands for a grand idea, but I doubt much if it is the idea which the social agitator has in mind when uttering his diatribes. Equity is probably what he means, for although justice is often used as synonymous with equity, each word has its own distinct shade of meaning.[1] If justice is what is aimed at, it may be well to remember that an absolutely

---

[1] "In its governmental relations, human or divine, *justice* is the giving to every person exactly what he deserves, not necessarily involving any consideration of what any other may deserve; equity (the quality of being equal) is giving every one as much advantage or privilege or consideration as is given to any other."—*James A. Fernald, "English Synonyms and Antonyms,"* p. 255.

equal division of the world's wealth might be farther from the line of strict justice than the division which obtains at present. "Every man according to his needs," is the cry of the social agitator; "Every man according to his works," is the dictum of eternal justice. A sober-minded socialist would probably say, "It is not an absolutely equal division that is demanded, but a more equitable one than now exists"; and to this I have no objection to offer. The present distribution of wealth is not only unequal, but from a purely worldly point of view it is inequitable. To a true citizen of the kingdom of God the problem has but little interest so far as he is personally concerned. He seeks first God's kingdom and righteousness, and whether he has much or little of this world's goods makes small difference, for, having food and raiment, he is therewith content. But if a more equitable division of existing wealth will relieve poverty, hush the clamor of rival interests, and bring in a reign of peace and contentment, he is quite willing to lend his influence in that direction, although there may be serious doubts as to whether the predicted results will follow.

Now the present unequal condition of affairs can be remedied in but one way—namely, by a redistribution, gradual or instantaneous, but made in such a way that the wealth will *stay* distributed, otherwise there would have to be repeated readjustments at short intervals. There are only three ways that I can think of in which a redistribution of existing wealth could be made: (1) By a series of voluntary surrenders on the part of those who have the wealth at present; (2) by violence, which is robbery; or (3) by law, which also *may* be robbery. A more equal distribution of life's comforts by voluntary surrender would not be out of harmony with the laws of the kingdom of God, but would be valuable just as it became general. A more equal distribution is what we will have some day, when the kingdom of God shall fill the earth; but it will take time, and many think it is too long to wait, even if the result were certain at the end of the waiting. Anarchism would adopt, I suppose, the second method, and redistribute wealth (by no means equally) by violence and barefaced robbery. The third method would be that of socialism pure and simple.

The present condition of society, that makes it possible for a limited number of persons to amass large possessions, while vast numbers have to content themselves with a modest living, and not a few with much less, may not be the best, but it would save much random talk if we would but remember that the condition of society at any particular period is never the result of a deliberate purpose on the part of society itself, but of ten thousand invisible causes, each of which has contributed in some measure to the general result. And even if society were responsible, in some tangible sense, for existing conditions, no change is conceivable that would render a return to those conditions *impossible*, albeit a general acceptance of the laws of Christ's kingdom would render that return unlikely. Here again it is man himself, not his condition, that needs to be changed, for "as long as there are inequalities in human character, they will show themselves in human condition."[1] Individual wealth on the one hand, and individual poverty on the other, show inequality, it is true, but inequality and injustice are not synonymous terms. If they were, nothing would be more unjust than the allotments of Providence, which, as far as human vision can see, are very unequal.

It is both misleading and mischievous to assume that the present condition of society, touching the distribution of wealth, is intentionally unjust, or that the accumulation of vast wealth by individuals necessarily implies dishonest or unfair methods.

---

[1] H. Watterson.

The foundations of many a large fortune have been laid by economy, industry, and thrift, at a time when the builder was comparatively poor; while the superstructure was reared by good judgment, energy, and enterprise; by the quick perception of opportunities, and the ability to seize them at the right moment. In all this there may be no injustice, no intention of wronging any one, and, indeed, no wrong done. It is freely admitted that present-day industrial and social conditions are far from being ideally the best; but the hope of making them so by legal enactments, without a great change in the moral character of men, is more Utopian than Utopia itself.

The epithets so freely hurled at capitalists, such as "exploiters of labor," "enslavers of labor," and the like, are not always or altogether without cause, but in many instances they are very unjust. The kings of industry who control large and varied interests, or those jugglers of finance whose Midas touch turns everything to gold, seldom—perhaps never—set out with the distinct purpose of oppressing the poor or of enslaving the world's toilers; but they follow the law of ambition and worship the goddess of success. They bow down (unconsciously, it may be) at the shrine of Mammon, and the oppression of the poor or the enslavement of labor are but incidents inseparable from pursuits that are based on selfishness. At the same time let us be just enough to admit that all capitalists and employers of labor are not unjust, nor is selfishness to be found only on that side. It has become the fashion to write and speak of the capitalist as though he were always a tyrant and an extortioner, and of the workingman as though he were always the innocent and helpless victim of the other's greed. But all this is untrue, and is mischievous in proportion as it is untrue. Are employers sometimes unjust? So are workmen. And the message of the gospel to both alike is: "Take heed, and beware of covetousness." For the evils complained of there is but one adequate remedy. Let employers and employed alike accept the laws of Jesus Christ as the standard of conduct in dealing with each other. This will put an end to strife by uprooting the selfishness which is at the bottom of it all.

When facing that problem which the world's ablest thinkers have vainly endeavored to solve—namely, such a distribution of wealth that each human being might have sufficient for his reasonable needs—the Lord Jesus announced a philosophy as startling as it was new, and summed it up almost in a sentence: "Be not therefore anxious for the morrow."[1] Experience teaches that much of the anxiety and unrest that embitter human lives arise from anticipations of trouble that never comes. If the average experience of men in this particular is to be our guide, rather than the laws of the kingdom of God, it seems as though we ought to add to some faculty in our universities a chair of hypothetics, which may be defined as the science of what might happen but does not. Take away from men the anxieties which arise from apprehensions of future trouble which may never come, and you relieve them of a large part of life's burdens and cares. And this is just what is blessedly true of those who have yielded heart and life to Jesus Christ, have become partakers of his Spirit, and are heirs of the kingdom of God. The laws of that kingdom forbid, and its rule in the heart makes impossible, all anxious and corroding care; and so with an undisturbed mind the children of the kingdom are able to "behold the birds of the air," and to "consider the lilies of the field." They are no more disquieted with thoughts of food and raiment, because their "heavenly Father knoweth that" they "have need of these things"; but, seeking "first the kingdom of God,

---

[1] Matthew vi. 34.

and his righteousness," they have the assurance that "all these things shall be added unto" them.[1]

In some parts of these discussions I have emphasized strongly—some may think too strongly—the earthward side of the kingdom of God, and the material benefits it was intended to confer. Let me guard the point by saying that these are not the only, or indeed the chief, benefits. This appears very clearly in Christ's own teaching, and nowhere more clearly than in an incident of his temptation in the wilderness. After his prolonged fast for forty days and forty nights, the pangs of hunger assailed him. Then came the tempter, saying: "If thou art the Son of God, command that these stones become bread."[2] To understand this we must take in the related circumstances. Jesus was just entering upon his work of establishing the kingdom of God in the world. This the tempter well knew, and to foil the attempt, if it were possible, was his settled purpose. To him the establishment of a spiritual kingdom in the heavens was nothing. That kingdom was already established, and nothing could shake it; but the kingdom of God in a world which Satan claimed as peculiarly his own was an altogether different

---

[1] Matthew vi. 25–32. [2] Matthew iv. 3.

matter. The temptation, then, was not a mere effort to induce the Saviour to commit a wrong act under the plea of supplying his own urgent needs, but to establish his kingdom on false foundations. It was as though the tempter had said: " If thou art the Son of God, whose kingdom shall be an everlasting kingdom, lay its foundations deep in the most universal need of humanity. Command that these stones become bread; and if thou canst do this to satisfy thine own hunger, thou canst do it to satisfy the hunger of the world. Begin thy kingdom by feeding the hungry. Abolish poverty, and all men will follow thee."

In his reply Jesus does not ignore this universal need of humanity, the hunger for bread, nor does he deny that the cure of poverty will be the outcome of his kingdom; but he recognizes the fact that humanity has other and greater needs which bread cannot supply, and that the abolition of poverty is to be brought about by other means than miraculous intervention. In other words, Jesus deals with poverty not as a disease but as a symptom of a disease which lies deeper in society than surface indications would imply; and he proposes to abolish poverty ultimately, in any sense in which it is an evil, by abolishing its causes. In the meantime poverty in the kingdom is to be dealt with as something to be relieved until such time as it can be entirely removed.

A twin grievance of the unequal distribution of wealth seems to be inequality of opportunity. We all know with what persistence the changes are rung on the "justice" of giving every man an "equal chance." An equal chance of what? one might ask, and the answers to the question may be manifold. The phrase may mean an equal chance of life and health; of food, clothing, and shelter; of obtaining remunerative employment; of securing an average share of the comforts and enjoyments of life, with the time and means and leisure necessary for mental culture, and a hundred things besides. But it matters little what the precise meaning of the phrase may be, for it proceeds upon a wrong assumption. The chances with which men begin life are not dependent upon human choice, and the most that can be done is to improve the chances when they are capable of improvement. Many men who start in life with chances as poor as they well can be, succeed, nevertheless, in almost everything they undertake; while others, who start with the best chances, either fail altogether or achieve only an indifferent success. If one thousand men could be taken at random from any rank or all ranks of society, and started with absolutely equal chances to-day, at the end of twenty or thirty years their positions will be as diverse as actually exist under the present social system. Nay, more; out of one thousand men, starting in life at the same time, with chances varying from the poorest to the best, before a generation has run its course some who had the best chances will be at the bottom of the hill, and some who had the worst chances will be at the top. The fact is, success in life depends not half so much upon having precisely equal chances with other people as upon the energy and persistence with which we seize and utilize the chances we have.

It is much to be deplored that this plaint of unequal chances has been petted and encouraged by not a few students of social ills as though it were perfectly legitimate, and as though "society" were to be blamed because every man's chances are not equal. In ancient times men were bolder. Instead of placing the blame upon "society," they placed it (with just as little justice) upon the Almighty, for they said: "The way of the Lord is not equal." The man who wastes his time complaining of unequal chances needs a good moral tonic, such as Jupiter is said to have given to the peasant whose cart stuck in the mire, and who cried loudly to the Thunderer to help him out; whereupon the god, looking down, bade him stop his shouting and, instead, put his shoulder to the wheel and whip up his horse.

Amid all this clamor about equal chances I shrewdly suspect that what is really desired is not an equal chance, but the results of chances which other people have utilized. Some man, we will suppose, has succeeded in life from the worldly point of view; he has amassed a fortune, lives in a fine mansion elegantly furnished, has carriages, servants, and every appliance that wealth can give. Success of this kind (we might almost say only of this kind) breeds envy, and envy is the parent of all uncharitableness. Not only is the man envied for what he has, but many who have not half his brains nor half his energy denounce him as a robber, an exploiter of labor, an oppressor of the poor; and being very desirous of reaching the same position by any road, provided it be an easy one, they are loud in their complaints that the Almighty, or society, or some other equally intangible power, has not given them an equal chance. This is bad enough, but it is made still worse when there is a chorus of cheap sympathy from a host of amateur social reformers, confirming the vicious, the improvident, and the willfully indolent in the delusion that they are a class of much-abused innocents that society is bound to pet and pamper.

Let us have done with this sentimental way of treating a serious problem, and learn to speak the truth, though the mob may hate it as of old, and cry, "Away with it! Crucify it!" Let men who pose as teachers of the people touching social duties have the courage of their convictions and say, what they know to be true, that by far the greater part of the social discontent of which we hear so much is the offspring of envy and covetousness, and that men are envious and covetous because they deliberately reject the teachings of Jesus Christ and trample on the laws of the kingdom of God. If we could but rid the world of the misery that is self-inflicted—if we could abolish the poverty that is the result of viciousness, indolence, intemperance, and unthrift—the rest could be easily reached and relieved. Far be it from me to teach, or even hint, that there is no real poverty to be relieved, no real sorrow to be comforted, no chances that need to be improved; but let us look honestly at the facts, so that we may not waste our very hearts in idle sentiment, our time in misdirected effort, our means in undeserved and misnamed charity.

What, then, is the duty of the Church or of society in this matter? It is to see that those without chances (if such there be), and able to use them, shall have a chance as soon as possible, and that those whose chances are very poor shall have better ones. But let us understand what this means. Neither society, nor the Church, nor the government, nor any individual or association of individuals, is under any obligation to find a man chances to become wealthy—to amass a fortune. All that God or man can justly demand of us is to see that each man or woman who can work, and is willing to do so, shall have a chance to earn an honest living, and receive enough for their labor to provide, at the very least, decent food, clothing, and shelter. But if society does this, it has a right to demand that such persons shall take any work that may be available, provided they have skill and strength to do it. But just here lies the heart of the difficulty. The army of incapables is enormous, and its ranks are recruited chiefly from among those who neglected chances when they had them and, Micawber-like, waited for better chances to turn up. The discouraging fact is that thousands who ask for work don't really want work; they want only a situation and a salary.

I do not say that it is the duty of society to furnish every man with *equal* chances; the first step is to see that he has *a* chance, and if he cannot or will not use it he must be dealt with in another way. To furnish some men with the best chances would only be to waste them. What we should try to reach in each man's case is the chance that is best for him. But the same chances are not the best for all. Some years ago the English colliers wanted a large increase of wages, so that they might have a chance of better living and greater home comforts. They got the increase, and the chances were fairly within their reach. The most obvious result, however, was the wholesale importation of champagne at three dollars a bottle, abounding drunkenness and debauchery, while the women and children starved on a pittance, with fewer home comforts than before. It may be said that a man has a right to a fair wage for his work, and society has no right to dictate what he shall do with it; but if society has to support him and his when out of work, as is often the case, then society has a very manifest right to inquire what he does with good wages when he has them.

LECTURE IV.—THE PROBLEM OF POVERTY.

"MODERN life," says a writer of the present day, "has no more tragical figure than the gaunt, hungry laborer, wandering about the crowded centers of industry and wealth, begging in vain for permission to share in that industry and to contribute to that wealth; asking in return not the comforts and luxuries of civilized life, but the rough food and shelter for himself and family which would be practically secured to him in the rudest form of savage society."[1] This picture is typical of what may be found in any crowded center of population, and it represents conditions which constitute one of the gravest problems of modern society. I do not affirm that it is in the power of the Church, or of any other association, to put an end to all poverty and the suffering which comes of it; that can be accomplished only when men universally accept and are governed by the precepts of Jesus Christ and are animated by his spirit; but I affirm that no such poverty as has just been described should ever be permitted to exist within the limits of the kingdom of God; and I further affirm that if the gospel code of social ethics is definitely accepted by the Church as a part of her working creed the time will come, and come soon, when no case of unrelieved poverty will be found among the followers of Jesus Christ. But before proceeding farther on this line it may be well to consider the problem itself.

---

[1] John A. Hobson, M.A., "Problems of Poverty," p. 17.

Poverty is a comparative term. What is regarded as poverty by very many persons in England and America would be regarded by millions in India or China as great comfort, if not as positive luxury. It is important, therefore, to determine just what is meant by poverty, and to what part of society the term "poor" may be properly applied. The question is not an easy one to answer. We cannot draw a broad line through society, and say the rich are on this side and the poor on that. Social conditions shade off gradually, and it is only when we compare extremes—the very rich with the very poor—that sharp contrasts appear. Perhaps by beginning at the top of the scale and coming downward we may reach a point below which all may be regarded as poor in the sense which makes poverty a problem of our civilization.

Owing to the rapid increase of the world's wealth, coupled with its unequal distribution, a considerable class have become very wealthy. They have accumulated to such an extent that they can live in luxury on a small percentage of the proceeds of their investments, and are constantly accumulating more. Such persons receive much from society without rendering any adequate service in return, unless, indeed, they belong to the limited class who regard wealth as a trust, and administer their large possessions for the common good. Then there is a large class who, partly by work of some kind and partly by income from accumulations, live in comfort, and have no need, so far as their circumstances go, to practice self-denial. Another very large class is composed of those whose income is derived from wages pure and simple, and whose savings, if any, are but small; nevertheless, so long as work is abundant and sickness does not intervene, they are able to provide all the necessaries of life, many of its comforts, and even some of its luxuries. Among these, however, in some branches of industry—and this is especially true of women and unskilled workers—competition is so keen, and the supply so much greater than the demand, that wages go down to a very low point; and this, together with periods of enforced idleness through sickness or lack of work, makes living exceedingly precarious. This brings us right among the poor; not the lowest strata, it is true, but among those whose poverty constitutes one of the phases of the problem.

Poverty, in many instances, is a misfortune to be relieved; in many more it is the offspring of idleness, unthrift, or dissipation, and these are vices to be corrected if possible; but there is a yet deeper form of poverty which, to an extent of which dreaming philanthropists are not aware, is a crime, and the prolific parent of crime, and which society, if only for its own protection, must quarantine and stamp out like an infectious disease. But before drastic remedies are applied we must be sure who is the criminal, lest society in its blindness should inflict punishment upon the wrong person. There is a great deal of deep poverty which implies criminality *somewhere*, but where? Sometimes, perhaps often, in the man himself. This statement covers probably nine-tenths of the chronic beggars and professional tramps who prey upon the industrious part of the community. They deliberately prefer their life of idleness, with its incidental exposure, hunger, and other disadvantages, to one of greater outward comfort won by honest labor; and no wonder, for they belong to a class which finds that preying upon society requires less exertion than would be required to earn a livelihood by daily toil; and although they pay a certain penalty by going clothed in rags and filth, and being without permanent shelter, yet the brute nature which a life of the kind so quickly develops reconciles them to these incidental disadvantages, especially when they discover that their chosen life frees them at a stroke from all duties and responsibilities as members of society, supplies them, as a rule, with something to eat and drink, which is about all they care for, and leaves them without a thought for the future as regards this life, and without feeling as regards a life to come. Pauperism of this type is a social disease so virulent that it cannot be cured by ordinary remedies, but requires a method of treatment peculiarly its own.

The causes of this kind of pauperism are many, and it would be impossible to trace the thousand and one influences which may lead to a result so fatal; but waiving for the present all considerations of heredity and environment, and an inveterate aversion to labor of every kind, it can scarcely be questioned that the chief causes are difficulty of obtaining steady employment, starvation wages, and the drink traffic. To these should be added another cause, though not so widely operative—namely, the case of those who have heedlessly, almost unintentionally, lapsed into what the law or society calls crime. They have committed some offense, made one false step; and then, finding no place of repentance, though they seek it diligently with tears—no kindly hand stretched out to help them to a better life—they sink step by step to the companionship of society's Ishmaelites, their hand against every man, and every man's hand against them. Now, while it is right that society should deal with the causes of pauperism, so far as to put an end, if possible, to a condition of affairs that is a reproach to our boasted civilization, it is no less important that the existing evil should be dealt with in some effective way. But how is this to be done? Beyond all cavil, existing methods are not effective; they do not touch the root of the mischief, and the evil is not diminished, but is on the increase. Among remedial measures the first step is an enlightenment of public opinion in several directions. The public has yet to learn that willful pauperism —the pauperism that comes of willing indolence or dissipation—is a crime against society, and should be punished as such. This class of social parasites should not be pampered and petted, but there should be a stern enforcement of that wholesome law of the kingdom of God, that "if any will not work, neither let him eat";[1] always provided, of course, that there is work for him to do and that he has strength to do it.

Just here the track we are following branches in two directions. We have to consider the case of those who will not work if they can help it, be work never so abundant, and also of those

---

[1] 2 Thessalonians iii. 10.

who would be glad to work if only they could get it to do. But these two classes cannot be dealt with alike. The first should be coerced, and the second should be aided. But how can coercion be applied? By finding something for the tramp or other social parasite to do, and then compelling him to do it. I do not advocate paternalism in government. The notion is mischievous from center to circumference, and wherever it shows itself should be firmly opposed. It has gained a broader foothold on this continent than many people are aware of, and is steadily reversing all just conceptions of the true relation of the citizen to the government. In former times the chief question with all patriotic citizens was: "What can we do for the government, to strengthen its hands, maintain its just authority, provide the necessary revenue for legitimate expenses, and help to enact laws in the interests of the whole people?" Now, to an ominously large extent, the question seems to be: "What can we induce the government to do for us, to provide us with offices and pensions, with fiat money to pay our debts and real money to expend lavishly in every locality, to make times easy when they are hard and work plentiful when it is scarce?" Government is regarded by multitudes as a kind of incarnate Providence, whose chief business is to say to the hordes of office seekers, contract seekers, needy and greedy politicians, distressed farmers, and the army of the unemployed: "Open your mouths wide, and I will fill them." The whole thing is wrong; the principle is vicious, and if it be allowed to prevail will tend to produce a whole nation of paupers, all gazing governmentward with open mouths, like a nest of robins waiting for the parent bird to drop in a worm. No plan could be devised more destructive to every element of true manhood, or more certain to result in a tyranny worse than we or our fathers ever knew.

But while holding firmly to this view, I think there are certain directions in which governmental interference might be helpful in solving the problem of poverty, especially in its worse forms. In a country like this, governments can set apart vast tracts of public lands for national parks and pleasure grounds. What hinders them from setting apart lands for industrial colonies, where the willing poor might get a chance to earn an honest livelihood, instead of leaving it to the Salvation Army or the like; and other colonies where, under strict discipline, the tramp and the social parasite might be compelled to contribute something to the productive power of the community, enough at least to cover the cost of their own support? Had this course been taken with Coxey and his army, not only would a dangerous tendency in modern society have been repressed, but assurance would have been given to the industrious and the law-abiding that government, even popular government, is something more than a figurehead.

There is another point on which the public, the Christian public especially, need to be enlightened—namely, that the maxim of the political economists which bids us "buy in the cheapest market, and sell in the dearest," is flatly antichristian. It breathes the spirit of that selfishness which is characteristic of the kingdom of this world, but is utterly and unalterably opposed to the kingdom of God. The application of this maxim is responsible for much of the suffering inflicted upon the poor. Investigations by a Royal Commission in England into what is called the "sweating system" revealed the fact that the worst sweating-master was the British public; and here is where another phase of the criminality of which I have spoken comes in. The craze for bargains—to buy at the lowest possible figure, without reference to the cost of production, and the consequent competition among tradesmen to lower prices at the expense of wages—has inflicted untold suffering and injustice upon workmen, and especially upon workwomen. The business house that appeals for patronage on the ground that it sells cheaper than any other is fairly open to the suspicion that it is defrauding the public by false representations, or defrauding the workers by lowering wages; for abnormally low prices for goods means abnormally low prices for producing them. The familiar legend, "Lowest prices charged here," should be replaced by another, "Highest wages paid here"; and wherever that is found to be true, there let the patronage of Christian men and women be given.

In order that we may get a clearer view of the relation of gospel ethics to this difficult social problem, let us try to ascertain just what is implied in the phrase so suggestive of the Saviour's mission: "The poor have the gospel preached unto them." The gospel is emphatically good news to all men, but what does it contain that makes it good news to the poor as distinguished from any other class? It is not a sufficient answer to say that it reveals a future state in which the poor shall be compensated for wrongs they have suffered here. The whole drift of gospel teaching shows that a man's future state will be determined, not by his social status in this world, but by his moral character; that he enters the kingdom of heaven, here or hereafter, not because he is poor in purse, but because he is poor in spirit. If, then, the gospel be good news to the poor, simply *as* poor, the explanation must be sought in the fact that it proclaims the definite advent of a kingdom in which poverty is no bar to citizenship, and in which poverty, with every disadvantage which that word implies, shall one day cease to be. I do not say that this is all the gospel, or even the chief part of it, but it is that part that makes it good news to the poor as such; and, as the fact that the poor had the gospel preached to them was a plain fulfillment of Isaiah's prophecy,[1] it is given by the Saviour as a crowning proof of his Messiahship.

If we follow the lines of the prophecy just referred to, and read it in the light of the New Testament, wherein Christ claims its fulfillment in himself, we shall find corroborative proof that the good news included the relief of human sufferings, the redress of human wrongs, and the establishment of justice and judgment in the earth, just as certainly as it included the regeneration of the individual and his preparation for heavenly felicity.

---

[1] Isaiah lxi. 1-3.

In Isaiah's prophetic announcement the Messiah is "anointed . . . to preach good tidings unto the poor,"[1] and the nature of the good tidings is outlined in the words that follow. He is "to bind up the broken-hearted, to proclaim liberty to the captives, and the opening of the prison to them that are bound; to proclaim the acceptable year of the Lord, and the day of vengeance of our God" upon the oppressor, and "to comfort all that mourn." If we turn now to the record in the Gospels, we shall see how these predictions had their fulfillment in the natural and literal, as well as in the spiritual and figurative, sense. There are two recorded occasions on which this prophecy was quoted by the Saviour: once in the synagogue at Nazareth,[2] and once when John the Baptist sent two of his disciples inquiring, "Art thou he that cometh, or look we for another?"[3] Instead of giving an immediate reply, Jesus "cured many of diseases and plagues and evil spirits; and on many that were blind he bestowed sight." Then he said to the messengers: "Go your way and tell John the things ye have seen and heard: the blind receive their sight, the lame walk, the

---

[1] Isaiah lxvi. 1 (marginal reading Revised Version).
[2] Luke iv. 16–19.
[3] Matthew xi. 3.

lepers are cleansed, and the deaf hear, the dead are raised up, the poor have good tidings preached to them."[1] These were the proofs of his Messiahship, and they all had reference to the present world except in so far as the good tidings preached to the poor may have included the grand spiritual truths of the kingdom.

At the present point the question may arise: If these things are so, and the kingdom of God in the earth is to be an everlasting kingdom, why are not the same works wrought to-day, and even on a grander scale? The words of Christ are very explicit: "Verily, verily, I say unto you, He that believeth on me, the works that I do shall he do also; and greater works than these shall he do; because I go unto the Father."[2] If these words are to be understood in their plain, obvious meaning (and I am unable to assign a reason why they should not be so understood), why is not the power to do these mighty works possessed in the Church to-day, especially when the Saviour's declaration is followed by another in these words, "Whatsoever ye shall ask in my name, that will I do, that the Father may be glorified in the Son,"[3] and in the light of the historic fact that the exer-

---

[1] Matt. xi. 4, 5. [2] John xiv. 12. [3] John xiv. 13.

cise of this power was not limited to the times of the apostles, but continued in the Church for the greater part of three centuries? One thing is certain: there is no hint in the teaching of Jesus that this gift was to be temporary; and if it has ceased, as must be admitted, the cause must be sought in the Church itself.

There are two sayings recorded in the Gospels which throw light upon the question. The first is contained in the words of Jesus to his disciples before he suffered: "If ye abide in me, and my words abide in you, ask whatsoever ye will, and it shall be done unto you."[1] The second is contained in the record of Christ's teaching at Nazareth, where it is said: "He could there do no mighty works, save that he laid his hands upon a few sick folk and healed them. And he marveled because of their unbelief."[2] In Matthew the record is still more emphatic, for it is said: "He did not many mighty works there because of their unbelief."[3] From these passages two things are clear: first, that abiding in Christ and the abiding of his word in us are indispensable conditions of answers to prayer; second, that a prevailing spirit of unbelief may be an insuperable hindrance to

---

[1] John xv. 7.   [2] Mark vi. 5, 6.   [3] Matthew xiii. 58.

the mighty works of Christ. Now, if it be true that certain great laws of the kingdom of God (such as the laws regarding property, class distinctions, and the like) have been so neglected that they have dropped out of the faith and almost out of the memory of the Church, and if it be true that the Church has been more or less leavened with the spirit and maxims of the world's unbelief, is it any wonder that the gift of which we are speaking has departed, and that the Church has been shorn of her strength? Beyond all dispute unbelieving men and women by thousands are in the Church to-day; they have brought in with them the worldliness, the pride, the ambition, the self-seeking which belong to the kingdom of this world, and while these remain unchanged they constitute a grievous hindrance to the mighty works of Christ. If any one doubts the prevalence of this kind of unbelief in the Church, let him propose in sober earnest that the words of Jesus touching these things of which I have spoken be accepted in their plain, obvious meaning, and obeyed, and even pious people and religious teachers will call him visionary, a dreamer, an enthusiast, a crank. But in spite of all this I cling to the hope that a day is coming when the words of Jesus will be thus accepted and obeyed;

and when that day comes, the power which the Church has lost will be restored.

Recalling the law of the kingdom of God touching property and its practical exemplification in the early Church, there are two things about it which I do not hesitate to affirm: first, there must be a return of the Church to this faith and practice before the grand ideal of the kingdom of God on the earth can be realized; and secondly, that the problem of poverty can be solved on this line and cannot be solved on any other. While the Church remained faithful in this respect, the problem was completely solved. For nearly three hundred years there was no poverty within the kingdom of God that was not quickly met and relieved, because it was an article of faith with those primitive believers that the average prosperity of each Christian community should extend to each individual member thereof when overtaken by any misfortune. More than this, the practice of accumulating or holding property beyond very moderate limits was regarded as characteristic of the kingdom of this world, but utterly foreign to the spirit of the kingdom of God.

In the course of the first two centuries the circumstances of the Christians changed greatly. Those habits of temperance, frugality, industry, and thrift which the gospel inculcated had improved their worldly circumstances, and there were whole communities where none were poor in the sense of needing assistance; but every call from presbyter or bishop for help to less fortunate communities ever met with a ready response, and even individual applications were rarely refused. The primitive Christians interpreted literally the words of Jesus: "Give to him that asketh thee, and from him that would borrow of thee turn not thou away."[1] They regarded their earthly possessions as belonging to God, and themselves as stewards intrusted with the management thereof. And as it is better to help a man out of his poverty than to help him in it, they regarded it as a part of their duty to find employment for every one able and willing to do something for the common good. Hence in the primitive Church none were idle save those who on account of age or infirmity were incapable of work.

If it should be said that such a system in our day would bring down upon every Christian home a swarm of tramps and paupers who would devour everything, one answer is that the early Christians found it not so. As long as the gospel principle

---

[1] Matthew v. 42.

was adhered to they prospered exceedingly, and the more they gave the more they had to give. Within the Church, as I have said, they solved the problem of poverty completely, while beyond the limits of the Church Christian benevolence relieved distress to an extent that is incalculable; and the same thing, as regards the latter point, is true to-day. It was only when the gospel principle was abandoned—when Christians, taking pattern from the kingdoms of this world, began to accumulate riches for their own use—that circumstances changed. Then the forces of poverty swooped down upon the Church and society like an armed host, creating problems which neither governments, nor poor laws, nor fraternal societies, nor insurance companies, nor any other appliance founded on Mammon worship, has yet been able to solve.

In all this the spirit and practice of the new kingdom was in marked contrast with the kingdoms of this world. In the latter the poor were not regarded as of any importance in the general scheme of society; they were regarded rather as an incumbrance, as a class having no rights which the more favored were bound to respect. In the kingdom of God all this was changed. Even in its incomplete development in Old Testament times the claims of the poor were recognized, and provision for their relief was regarded as a religious duty; but no plan ever emanated from heathen governments for the relief of human suffering or for improving the condition of the common people. It was reserved for the kingdom of God to recognize and act upon the principle that within the limits of the kingdom there should be no poverty or suffering that the most absolute consecration of property or personal service could relieve; and if in obedience to this principle the follower of Christ gave without reserve of his substance to feed the poor, it was not because the law of the kingdom said you *must*, but because the love of Christ said you *can*, and enlightened conscience said you *ought*.

In the primitive Church the phrase "communion of saints" meant something more and something far different than it means in modern creeds. It meant not only spiritual fellowship, but such communion of property rights as made it impossible for the humblest believer to suffer for lack of food or raiment. The Church was a partnership administered on the principle of equal rights, and this is the very thing which men are now trying to bring about in society by methods which must inevitably frustrate the end in view. Nay, almost ever since this feature of Christianity was subverted in the fourth century, men have been trying to find a substitute—first by monastic institutions founded on a communistic basis, later by means of legal enactments and benevolent associations, and now by Christless forms of secular communism and socialism, or a vindictive nihilism which threatens the very existence of law and order.

There are two ways of helping a poor man: one is to help him *in* his poverty, the other is to help him *out* of it; or, better still, to show him how to help himself out of it. The first is the way of "charity," so called; the second is the way of New Testament Christianity. There is no more striking proof of the extent to which the Church has diverged (unwittingly, I fain would hope) from the New Testament ideal than the universality with which Christian people suppose that the so-called charity of to-day is synonymous with that love of the brethren which Christ inculcated, and which Paul enthroned as the cardinal virtue and the crowning grace. Charity, as commonly understood, holds much the same relation to love that a counterfeit holds to a genuine coin. To solve the world's social problems (preëminently the problem of poverty) two things are essential, namely, brotherhood and stewardship; and these, to be of any real value, must have their source in a regenerated nature, "the love of God shed abroad in the heart by the Holy Ghost."

Next to the difficulty of obtaining steady employment, starvation wages take rank as a cause of deep poverty. It is contended by a certain school of economists that labor is like any other commodity, and that its value is regulated by the law of supply and demand; that when labor is abundant wages go down, and when it is scarce wages rise. The principle is false as well as selfish. Work cannot be separated from the human beings who perform it, and human souls and bodies are not commodities to be bought in the cheapest possible market. Selfishness may condone such a practice; but righteousness repudiates it, and righteousness is the very foundation of the kingdom of God. Perhaps there is no one way in which professing Christians have brought so much reproach upon the Church of God as by this sin of oppressing the hireling in his wages; and the fault cannot be atoned for by munificent gifts to charitable objects. We are to "do justly" as well as to "love mercy," and in the order of virtues justice comes first. After justice is done we can be as generous as we please.

THE PROBLEM OF POVERTY. 163

Doubtless it is better that a man have employment at small wages than not to be employed at all, but that does not touch the requirements of justice as regards the employer. He has no right to take advantage of a workman's necessities, and reduce wages because the labor market is overstocked, to offer starvation wages because a dozen persons are competing for a piece of work. In any case the minimum wage should be enough to maintain in reasonable comfort the workman and those depending upon him; and if there is difficulty in deciding just how much that ought to be, it might assist in solving the problem if every employer would ask himself the question, "What would I consider fair were the case reversed, and I were the workman?" For this is only an indirect way of applying the fundamental law of the kingdom of God: "All things therefore whatsoever ye would that men should do unto you, even so do ye also unto them: for this is the law and the prophets."[1]

---

[1] Matthew vii. 12.

LECTURE V.

LABOR DISPUTES, AND HOW TO END THEM.

"How is this growing wealth divided? Is it rightly or wrongly divided? If it is wrongly divided, has the Christian moralist anything to say about a better way? Christianity, as we have seen, has much to do with the production of wealth; has it anything to do with its distribution?" (Washington Gladden, "Applied Christianity," p. 9.)

"Every approximation toward a community of goods should be affected by the love of the rich for the poor, and not by the hatred of the poor for the rich. If all men were true Christians, a community of goods might exist without danger. But then, also, the institution of private property would have no dark side to it. Every employer would give his workmen the highest wages possible, and demand in return only the smallest possible sacrifice." (Professor Rocher, quoted in "Applied Christianity," p. 22.)

(It should be added that, "if all men were true Christians," not only would "every employer give his workmen the highest wages possible," but every workman would render the best and most faithful service possible.—A. S.)

"I believe that in the adoption of the philosophy of the religion of Jesus Christ as a practical creed for the conduct of business lies the surest and speediest solution of those industrial difficulties which are exciting the minds of men to-day, and leading many to think that the crisis of government is at hand." (Carroll D. Wright.)

"All things therefore whatsoever ye would that men should do unto you, even so do ye also unto them: for this is the law and the prophets." (Jesus, Matt. vii. 12.)

V.
PRELUDE.—THE CHURCH AND WORKINGMEN.

JESUS CHRIST—I speak it with reverence—was a workingman; his kingdom was founded among workingmen; his first ministers were workingmen; a large part of the world's population are workingmen. If, therefore, the Church is in any measure identical with the kingdom which Christ came to establish, and desires to be true to its origin and divine ideal, there should be everything in the Church to attract the world's toilers, and nothing to repel them. But is this the case? Are workingmen attracted to the Church in the present day as they were to Jesus Christ when "the common people heard him gladly"? The most pronounced optimist will scarcely venture to affirm that they are. At the same time I cannot bring myself into sympathy with extremists who declare that there is a mighty chasm between the Church and workingmen that never can be bridged over. The statement has a measure of truth when applied to the unchurched masses of the old world, and to considerable numbers in the great centers of population on this continent; but it is an utter exaggeration when applied to the working population as a whole. But although there is as yet no broad chasm, there is a narrow rift, and unless timely steps are taken this may widen until it becomes a "great gulf fixed," too deep to be fathomed and too wide to be crossed. It will be far easier to close the rift now than to bridge the chasm fifty years hence.

The Church and the workingmen ought to be firm friends and allies. Alienation of confidence and sympathy, leading to antagonism, would be an unspeakable calamity to both. The workingmen have need of the Church, and the Church has need of the workingmen. Rather let me say, the workingmen should *be* the Church. It was theirs at the first; and if they have suffered it to slip out of their hands, the duty of the hour is to claim back their inheritance and insist that the Church shall be what Jesus intended it to be—bread for the hungry, clothing for the naked, protection for the friendless, a refuge for the oppressed; above all, that it should be the one place where arbitrary social distinctions shall disappear, and where, on the foundation of a common brotherhood, rich and poor shall meet together, acknowledging that God is the Maker and Father of them all.

I do not think that any real antagonism exists between the Church and the workingmen as such, but only with that class (a small one, I hope) of skeptical and irreligious men who antagonize all religion, or that other class who make the assumed delinquencies of the Church an excuse for the habitual neglect of religion. The fact that in every Christian congregation workingmen are to be found, sometimes constituting the bulk of the membership, is proof positive that there is no insuperable barrier between the two. Multitudes of workingmen have found in the Church a congenial spiritual home, and are not slow to acknowledge the benefits derived from the association. At the same time there are vast numbers of working people, neither skeptical nor irreligious in any strong sense of those terms, who are not in cordial sympathy with the Church, who stand aloof from it to the mutual disadvantage of the Church and themselves. If this is true, it is a serious matter, and demands serious attention in regard to both cause and cure.

Such antagonism as does exist between the Church and a certain class of workingmen is not to be altogether accounted for on the ground of natural depravity or the enmity of the carnal mind. Neither would it be wise to assume that the blame is all on one side. The alienation of sympathy which does exist is due to causes for which neither party is entirely responsible. There has not been any violent reaction on the part of workingmen against religious teaching as such, nor any supercilious "passing by on the other side" on the part of the Church; but gradually a feeling of estrangement has crept in, as though the interests of the workingmen were entirely distinct from those of the Church, and could not be combined. This has arisen, in part, from the growing wealth of some, and consequent changes in social position. The thoughts of the average workingman run in one channel, those of the successful business or professional man run in another; and this tends to produce a class feeling, which sometimes shows itself in the Church as well as out of it. Nor is there anything which can overcome this tendency save that unfeigned Christian sympathy which recognizes the real brotherhood of all believers in Christ Jesus.

Another cause of the lack of sympathy for the Church on the part of workingmen is the old strife between capital and labor. Strictly speaking, there can be no strife between capital and labor—they are natural partners and allies, and the one is comparatively useless without the other; but there has been strife between capitalists and laborers, and as capitalists are sometimes members of the Church, not a few laborers have jumped to the conclusion that the Church on the whole is on the side of the capitalist. I do not regard the conclusion a just one, but the deference sometimes paid by the Church to wealthy men has given grounds for the suspicion that she is not altogether free from the sin of having "respect of persons." Moreover, the relative rights and duties of employers and employed are questions on which the pulpit is usually silent; and thus the very person to whom the workingman should naturally look as his friend and champion is regarded as neutral at the best, if not positively unfriendly. From all this it comes to pass that, although the Church may have ready welcome for all who come within her pale, and does what she can to minister to their spiritual needs, the conviction exists that she holds herself aloof from the struggles and aspirations of workingmen as a class; that she does not champion the cause of the poor against the rich, or the weak against the strong; and thus the workingman is led to seek in trades unions and fraternal societies the sympathy and moral support which he does not always find in the Church.

Among the minor causes which keep many workingmen aloof from the Church are such as the following: "The churches are too fine for ordinary working people to attend." "The system of renting pews at high figures puts churchgoing beyond our means." "Average churchgoers dress so finely that we feel out of place among them in our common clothes." And last, but not least, "When we do go to church no one takes any notice of us; we do not feel as if we were made welcome, and do not care to go again." Now, admitting that there is some truth in all this; admitting that it might have been better if the various denominations had not built so many costly churches, burdened with heavy debts, necessitating high pew rents and many other evils; admitting that costly raiment is not only out of place in the house of God, but that it shames the face of the poor; admitting that with most of us there is a foolish reserve which hinders us from giving a welcome to the stranger within our gates that will make him feel entirely at home; admitting that all these hindrances exist in some measure, yet the experience of those who are in the Church shows that they are not insurmountable, and that, as hindrances, they are larger in imagination than in reality. The chief difficulty here, as elsewhere, is in the man himself; for, no matter what may have been his complaints against the Church, no matter how strong his dislike of its ministers, teachings, or methods, only let that great spiritual change pass upon him which we call conversion, but which Jesus calls being born from above, and instantly suspicion, dislike, antagonism, vanish away; his complaints are hushed, and in the Church, which once he hated and despised, he finds a congenial spiritual home.

In seeking to promote more cordial relations between the Church and workingmen it is essential that the representative men of the Church—the ministers and influential members—should learn to look at a great many questions from the workingman's point of view, and thus, as it were, put themselves in his place. And this is the more important because not a few who claim to speak on behalf of workingmen do not always fairly state their views. We must learn to distinguish between the glib utterances of the labor agitator and the deep and often unuttered feelings of the average workingman. To accomplish this, the wisest and best men in the Churches should seek to mingle with the workingmen in their places of business, in their homes, in their association meetings (where that is possible), with a sincere desire to learn their needs, to help in their struggles, to sympathize with their aspirations and hopes.

In the next place, the Church needs to learn what this meaneth, of "Man shall not live by bread alone"; no, nor even by religion alone. No one thing—not even religion—can fill the whole round of man's needs, and the Church must learn to champion the cause of the toiling masses in regard to many things which lie outside of the spiritual realm. She has done what she could to teach men those truths of religion which relate to inward experiences and a future state, and has not been unmindful of the great rules of personal morality outlined in the decalogue; but the broad domain of social ethics has been until recently a virtually unexplored territory. Touching the wide range of man's social needs, we have too often said, like the disciples at Bethsaida, "Send the multitudes away"; and where this has been the case we have no right to complain if many of them have taken us at our word, and have gone away to their lodge rooms and their trades unions for the things they needed but could not find in the Church. The Church must correct this. She must make the world's workers see that she is their stanch friend in everything that is "true, and lovely, and of good report"; and that all they need of sympathy, of encouragement, of coöperation for the promotion of their intellectual, industrial, social, and spiritual interests, they can find in the Church of Jesus Christ.

Let it not be supposed that nothing has been done in this direction. In great centers of population, like London and New York, agencies for the relief of poverty, and for the educational, moral, and social advancement of the working classes are multiplying every day. One of the most notable of these agencies had its origin in the universities. Groups of refined and cultured men and women have gone into the poorest quarters of London and New York, not to distribute condescending charity, but to live right among the poorest people, sharing their sorrows, sympathizing in their trials, opening avenues of hope for the future, showing the way to a better life here and hereafter. Speaking of such work in the East End of London, a recent writer observes: " Hence have come Toynbee Hall, with its sane and sagacious belief in the value of art for the squalid East End, and its brave endeavor to educate the university by means of Whitechapel, and to save Whitechapel by the culture and service of the universities; Oxford House, with its intense conviction of the mission of the Church to the masses, though of a mission that the ordinary ecclesiastical agencies and methods are quite unable to fulfill;" Mansfield House, with its strong practical spirit, seeking to improve the houses, the amusements, the minds, the relationships, and the lives of the workers in the farther East End; the Wesleyan Settlement at Bermondsey, with its noble religious zeal and broad philanthropy, attempting at once to heal the bodies and save the souls of those it can reach; University Hall, with its intellectual energy and its belief in knowledge as a saving and civilizing power; and besides these, a multitude of houses and missions independently and separately maintained by colleges and public schools." [1]

And these are but samples of countless Christian agencies that are at work all over the world for the moral, social, intellectual, and spiritual uplifting of the race. Notwithstanding all that has been said in disparagement of the Church and its work, it remains true that in all that has yet been done for the betterment of human conditions, especially those of the poor and the toilers, the Church of God has been the most potent factor.

But if workingmen desire the friendship and coöperation of the Church, there is something for

---

[1] Principal Fairbairn, "The Church and the Working Classes," p. 3.

them to consider. If the workingman has a claim upon the Church, the Church has a claim upon the workingman. Let mutual duties and responsibilities be recognized, and the way to coöperation is made plain. It is most important, too, that Christian workingmen who desire to promote harmony and good will between the Church and the laboring classes should learn to speak for themselves, instead of being spoken for, as they often are, by irreligious and even skeptical men, whose real object is not to heal the breach, but to widen it. To sum up, let me repeat that the workingman needs the Church, and the Church needs the workingman. There is every reason why they should be close friends and allies, none why they should be strangers, much less foes. Let them approach each other with mutual confidence and respect, talk over their differences, if such there be, unite their efforts for the promotion of right and the suppression of wrong, and we may rest assured the time is not far distant when it will be felt and seen that the workingman's best friend is the Church, and that the Church's best friend is the workingman.

LECTURE V.—LABOR DISPUTES, AND HOW TO END THEM.

Perhaps the most difficult problem confronting the kingdom of God on the earth is found in the social movements and industrial complications of the times. That there is almost universal unrest among the toiling millions, is a fact too apparent to be questioned. That this unrest implies dissatisfaction with existing social conditions, is equally plain; and it may also imply, as many affirm, a growing determination, on the part of working-men, to demand and secure what they conceive to be their rights, peaceably if they can, by violence if they must. The signs of the times make it clear that the conflict between capital and labor is not ended. The very fact that such a conflict exists shows that something is wrong, for in the nature of things capital and labor, being mutually dependent upon each other, should be allies and not antagonists. This growing unrest; these plaints of injustice, whether well founded or not; this craving for a larger share of the world's wealth and a more abundant supply of its creature comforts, whether honestly earned or not; this idea, so persistently drummed into the ears of the toilers, that all poverty and distress are the outcome of injustice and oppression on the part of the wealthy, are all prophetic of embittered conflicts between class and class that may shake the social fabric to its foundations. And the chief danger lies in this: that unrest and discontent afford the political demagogue and the professional agitator an opportunity, which they eagerly seize upon, to delude and mislead the toiling masses by holding up false and exaggerated pictures of the injustice and tyranny of wealth, and dangling before their eyes pictures of impossible millenniums to be ushered in when wealth is equally divided and a dreary uniformity of condition is enforced by law. But admitting this to be true, it may still be said that something is wrong. Yes, something *is* wrong. Human nature is wrong—just as wrong in the poor man as in the millionaire; and this is precisely the factor that is left out of account by Utopian dreamers who would have us believe that millenniums can be manufactured to order simply by changing a man's environment, although his inner nature is left untouched and unchanged. But of this we may rest assured, that a society that is morally wrong can never be made right by political machinery. The reform must begin from within. Make the man right, and his social conditions will soon be rectified; leave him the slave of his natural selfishness, and every change in his environment will only aggravate the evils they seek to cure.

There is no more striking proof of the craft and cunning of Satan than the ease with which he sets men to chasing shadows, while the substance lies neglected within their reach. Thus, instead of each man setting himself to improve his own conditions and mend his own morals, they start in pursuit of millenniums that they think can be reached without the subjugation of human passions or the cure of human selfishness. What marvel that the chase always ends in disappointment, and is followed by deeper discontent than before? And yet this very discontent has in it an element of hope, for it serves to show that out of God in Christ there is no rest for the human soul. And it may be that when tariff millenniums, and fiat money millenniums, and single-tax millenniums, and socialistic millenniums, and looking-backward millenniums shall have vanished like the mirage of the desert, the disappointed and sorrowing hearts of men may turn wistfully toward that real millennium, foreshadowed in prophecy and in gospel, when society shall be reconstructed because its units have been regenerated, and social conditions shall be equalized because human hearts have been renewed, and righteousness shall reign because Christ is enthroned, and the social justice of which men have dreamed, but have seen only in their dreams, shall be found at last in the divine charity that "seeketh not her own."

What, then, ought to be the attitude of the Church, and what her duty, as she stands on the shore of this ocean of seething unrest? Is it to look on with stolid indifference while the strife becomes more bitter? Is it to stand on the demagogue's platform and shout herself hoarse in the teeth of the human hurricane? Has she no oil to cast on the troubled waters, no voice of power to hush the tumult to calm? Has she no message of help and hope for the "submerged tenth" as they struggle and sink beneath the flood? If not, it were as well to confess at once that the Christianity of to-day is but a shadow of its divine original. But, thank God! there is no call for a confession so humiliating. The Church has a message to all classes and conditions of men which, if heeded, will solve industrial and social as well as religious problems, and she must not withhold it at a time like this. But her message is too important and her mission too broad to allow her to lean on any party, or to champion any industrial combine among either master or men. Her great need just now is for men who have time and ability to master social problems; who can stand unmoved amid the surgings of human passion and breast the angry waves of popular excitements; who amid the clamor for a larger share of the world's wealth fear not to affirm that man cannot live by bread alone, and that to teach the contrary, as is done by the demagogue and the dreamer, is to deny God and degrade man; that social problems, in their last analysis, are not questions of private wages or public finance, of government groceries or single tax, but the far more difficult question of selfish human nature, so insistent upon what it considers to be its own rights that it has no thought to spare for the rights of others. Above all does the Church need men who can tell out, in "thoughts that breathe and words that burn," that there is but one way of solving industrial problems and ending industrial disputes, and that is the acceptance, by masters and men alike, of the law of Christ—the golden rule—and its application to the affairs of the countinghouse and the factory, as well as to the Church and the home. This is the solution of all problems, the answer to all questions, the prophecy of all the ages, and the only hope of the world.

Let no one say that this view is Utopian; that few will listen to it or be influenced by it. It is true there was a time when the appeal of men everywhere, on every subject touching human welfare in this life, was to Cæsar, and there are many still who think that in civil government and its machinery lies the only hope of society; but this trend of thought is changing, and more and more the appeal is to Jesus the Christ. Once it was supposed that his teachings had reference solely to an invisible state, and to mystical experiences in an invisible realm, where few could follow him with any satisfying assurance of certainty; but now, in regard to the problems of the present life, there is a large and increasing number who are turning Christward, saying, "We know that thou art a teacher come from God"; and they are joining to swell the cry that may be the watchword of the not distant future, "Back to Christ!" Still it must be confessed that even in this apparent movement of human thought Christward there lurks a danger of no ordinary magnitude. There is a tendency among men who are not in the least degree in sympathy with the spirit and laws of the kingdom of God to make Christ a stalking-horse for every new fad and crude theory in social economics. That Christ was a socialist is confidently affirmed by men whose socialism has nothing in common with the gospel of the kingdom which he proclaimed; and there is scarcely a social iniquity, from divorce to free love and Mormonism, which does not try to pervert his gospel into a seeming acquiescence, or a wild scheme for the reconstruction of society which does not claim to find its justification in some principle which he taught. This stealing of the livery of heaven in which to serve the devil is no new thing under the sun; but the Church of God must plant itself immovably upon this ground, that Christ is man's Leader and Helper in holiness, not his partisan in strife, much less his apologist in wickedness; that the foundation principles of his kingdom strike at the root of all selfishness and injustice alike in individual character and in social organization, and that before we can claim his indorsement or help there must be an absolute surrender of our opinions to his teachings, of our hearts and lives to his control, and of our plans for the reconstruction of society to the recognized laws of the kingdom of God.

While holding that the laws of the divine kingdom regulate, by broad general principles, everything that relates to property and to man's social relations, I do not mean that the Church was constituted by its Founder a court of arbitration in property or labor disputes. Indeed, the contrary may be inferred, for when one appealed to the Master, saying, "Bid my brother divide the inheritance with me,"[1] the answer was prompt and decisive: "Who made me a judge or a divider over you?"[2] And then, striking at the root of all property and labor disputes, he adds: "Take heed and keep yourselves from all covetousness: for a man's life consisteth not in the abundance of the things which he possesseth."[3] Similar conditions prevail in the world to-day; for, although the form of the demand has changed, the principle is the same. Once it was, "Bid my brother divide the inheritance with me"; now it is, "Bid my employer divide the profits with me." But if Christ could not be a judge in such matters, neither can his Church, and there are good reasons why it should not attempt it. There are multitudes who would be glad to have the Church cast its influence into the scale in the conflict between capital and labor, with a view to obtaining a more equal division, who have not the slightest intention of submitting themselves to the laws of the divine kingdom or of helping to extend its sway. The first duty of the Church is not to judge, but to teach and exemplify those great truths of the

---

[1] Luke xii. 13.   [2] Luke xii. 14.   [3] Luke xii. 15.

kingdom of God which end disputes by eradicating the covetousness from which they spring.

Social and industrial problems admit of no solution along the line of mere human enactments so long as the laws of the kingdom of God are disregarded. Such enactments cannot touch the seat of the mischief, which lies deep in the nature of man. Much less is it possible to solve them by brute force. Such methods only aggravate the passions in which human wrongs have their origin and from which they derive their strength. It follows, therefore, that if the laws of the kingdom of God are to control Christian men in their conduct toward their fellow-men they can give no countenance to violent strikes or boycottings on the one hand, or to lockouts on the other, as a means of settling labor disputes. The gospel not only forbids all violent and coercive measures, but it equally opposes the enforcement of personal rights and the revenging of injuries. In the kingdom of this world it is not so. There the ruling policy is to enforce personal rights at all hazards; to return blow for blow; to demand "an eye for an eye, a tooth for a tooth"; to seize the defaulting servant by the throat with an imperative "Pay me that thou owest"; and if he will not or cannot pay, then to inflict as much punishment upon him as the laws of the kingdom of this world will allow. But Jesus teaches the very reverse of all this, and hence to bring the laws of both kingdoms to bear in the settlement of labor disputes is a simple impossibility. The disputants must choose between the two; and as human laws have not yet ended the strife between capital and labor, but rather have aggravated its bitterness, it would now seem to be in order to try the other method.

At a mass meeting composed chiefly of working people, I heard a female speaker begin her address with the words: "Has labor *rights?* has labor *wrongs?*" Of course both questions were answered in the affirmative, and I have no disposition to quarrel with the answer. It is quite true that labor has rights, and it may be equally true that labor has wrongs, and all Christian men should lend a hand to concede the one and redress the other. But the speaker did not go far enough. She should have asked the further questions, "Has labor *duties?* has labor *responsibilities?*" and she should have been brave enough to say that, unless labor tries honestly to perform its duties and meet its social responsibilities, it cannot with so good a grace demand concession of rights or redress of wrongs. Then she might have added that some of the wrongs from which labor suffers are self-inflicted, at least in part, and that so long as labor makes little or no effort to free itself of ills that are real and curable it cannot well complain if society at large does not grow enthusiastic over wrongs that are half imaginary. Still further it should be said that this is not wholly a one-sided question. Capital has its rights (and possibly its wrongs) as well as labor, and this should be remembered in all attempts to adjust their mutual relations.

Recognizing the existence of widespread social discontent, we should not shut our eyes to the fact that it is by no means universal, even among the wage-earning class. It is found chiefly in the cities, rarely in the country towns; and it should not be forgotten that in nearly all great social and political movements it is the country vote that tells. As a recent writer has tersely expressed it, "the provinces are not yet prepared to upset the present industrial scheme on the chance that a few desperate agitators, with a smattering of knowledge, backed by an intrepid vanity, may instantly provide a better."[1] Recent politico-social movements in some of the western states of the American republic may seem to contradict this view, but as the same writer remarks, "there is a very common

---

[1] Octave Thanet, in *Forum*, October, 1894, p. 204.

belief that the West is in a sullen revolt against the present, and willing to turn its hand to any vagary in finance or sociology. But this is true not of the West, but only of limited portions of the West"; [1] and where it does obtain it has been due not to labor disputes, but to agricultural depression and exceptional financial conditions. As a rule, the social agitator and the walking delegate have little chance with the workmen in country towns. The latter, very often, are men who have saved something, own their own homes perhaps, have a stake in the community; and if they are industrious and sober, are respected accordingly. They are regarded as men and as citizens—influential members of the body politic; whereas workingmen who mass themselves in great cities are in danger of sinking into the position of mere cogs in an industrial machine, to be manipulated by the politician and the demagogue for their own selfish ends. While labor in many of the great cities is in a condition of seething unrest, its condition in country towns is not inaptly represented by the replies of two mechanics in an Iowa town during the great railway strike. The remark was made: "You have not struck, I see." "Struck?" replied one of

---

[1] Octave Thanet, in *Forum*, October, 1894, p. 204.

them. "I guess it would be like hunting for a needle in a haystack to find a man who has struck in this town. We ain't that kind of fools." When it was suggested that there were not many union men in the place, another mechanic replied: "I guess that's right; but all the same there's not a town in the country where more workingmen own their own houses or where there's more workingmen's money in the savings bank or invested in shares in factories." When similar results can be shown in places where trades unionism is in the ascendant, it will do more to attract and hold the sympathy of thoughtful citizens than a hundred strikes, with their attendant miseries, ordered by some irresponsible labor autocrat.

All discontent should not be denounced as though it were evil and only evil. There is a kind of discontent which is a necessary condition of all progress. People who are perfectly contented with their circumstances, their attainments, their prospects, will never advance a hair's breadth, socially or otherwise. Then there is another kind which springs from the perversity of human nature, and this is precisely the kind which neither social nor political revolutions nor change of circumstances can ever cure. If all its desire were granted to-day, it would be as clamorous as ever over some new grievance to-morrow. But there is still another kind of discontent—or let us say, dissatisfaction—found chiefly among various classes of wage-earners, with which every Christian man must sympathize where the alleged causes really exist, and it has reference to such things as these: uncertainty of employment, or difficulty of obtaining it; insufficient pay and, as a consequence, insufficient food, clothing, and shelter; a very unequal share of life's comforts; and no leisure nor means for improvement or recreation. Put into other words, the discontent among the industrial classes voices itself in the demand for (1) steady employment, (2) shorter hours, (3) better pay; and each of these demands is deserving of serious and sympathetic consideration. But as the first demand belongs to the problem of poverty, and has been discussed in that connection, we may confine our observations to the other two.

Whether a demand for shorter hours is just or not may depend upon a variety of considerations. The number of hours which is supposed to constitute a working day is not the same in all places or in all kinds of labor. As a rule, it is the unskilled laborer that has to work the longest hours for the smallest pay; and this in turn is due to the fact that almost everywhere, but especially in the cities, the supply of unskilled or low-skilled labor is largely in excess of the demand. As we ascend the scale, the higher the skill required the shorter the hours or the better the pay—one or both. Then again the nature of the work to be done should have something to do in determining the hours. Some kinds of labor are exceedingly fatiguing, and the expenditure of vital force is very great; others again are unhealthy, and have to be carried on amid unhealthy surroundings. In all these the hours of consecutive work should be brought within narrow limits. Where work is light and healthful, hours may be extended without injury as far as the physical condition of the worker is concerned, but even here there should be a reasonable limit. In determining what is a reasonable limit there is difficulty on both sides. There are employers who will exact all the hours to which workmen can be compelled to submit; and workmen who will give just as few hours as the employer can be induced to accept. The gospel law, if allowed to prevail, would correct all this; for then the employer and the workman, instead of considering how they can outwit and take advantage of each other, will consider how they can best help each other and promote each other's interests, and this would quickly result in an adjustment respecting both hours and wages that would go far to end disputes. The real trouble is that the whole industrial system under present conditions is carried forward on a war footing, and the best that seems practicable is an armed truce between employers and employed that at any moment may end in fresh hostilities. In this contest perhaps neither party is entirely to blame. "No man," says Carlyle, "at bottom means injustice; it is always for some obscure distorted image of a right that he contends; an obscure image diffracted, exaggerated in the wonderfulest way, by natural dimness and selfishness, getting tenfold more diffracted by exasperation of contest, . . . yet still the image of a right."

The demand for better pay, like that for shorter hours, cannot be settled by an *ipse dixit*, but must be judged, to some extent at least, by circumstances. "A fair day's wage for a fair day's work" sounds well, but after all it is only a very inconclusive truism, the force of which depends on the answer to two other questions, namely, What *is* a fair day's wage? and What *is* a fair day's work? Waiving, for the present, a specific answer to these two difficult questions, it may be said in general terms that the prevailing rate of wages, in most branches of productive industry, does not represent a fair return for the labor bestowed. It is beyond dispute that within the last hundred years the world's wealth, or rather the wealth of Christian nations, so called, has gone up by leaps and bounds; but the condition of skilled labor — one of the chief factors in producing this increased wealth — shows only moderate improvement; the condition of unskilled labor, little improvement at all; while the condition of the very poor is relatively worse than before. In other words, the result, thus far, of the present industrial system has been a fabulous increase of wealth at one end of the social scale, with grinding poverty and untold suffering at the other; and with such a tremendous object lesson before us, one has no difficulty in reaching the conclusion that in the distribution of the world's rapidly growing wealth capital has received far more than its equitable share, and labor far less. Now while there is nothing in the ethical code of the New Testament requiring an equal division of profits as between employer and employed, there is much in that code as to how wealth should be used by those into whose hands it may fall; and even an ordinary conception of what is just and right as between man and man should be sufficient to show that the first duty of the man who is growing rich on the products of labor is to see that an equitable share is assigned to those out of whose labor his profits have chiefly been made. Self-interest, to speak of no higher motive, should dictate this course; for "it is admitted by every economist of note that underpayment of labor results at once in inefficient labor and in diminished power of production."[1]

While adhering firmly to the proposition that the social ethics of the New Testament alone can solve the industrial problems of the times, it would be unwise to expect a sudden and universal acceptance of that code as the basis of industrial relations throughout the world. The kingdom of God is like the seed that groweth secretly, or the leaven that works silently and unobserved in the meal; and we must look for its gradual extension rather than for some swift and sudden transformation of society. But in the meantime much may be done to lead men to test the ethics of the gospel in the conduct of business affairs; and if it should be found, as undoubtedly will be the case, that they furnish an infinitely better basis than the selfish maxim of the *laissez faire* school of economists for the adjustment of human relations, the way will then be open for their universal acceptance and application. There are certain principles that

---

[1] A. Scott Matheson.

might and should be applied forthwith. First of all, both capital and labor should assume—and act upon the assumption—that so long as their attitude is one of mutual and bitter antagonism there can be no equitable settlement of labor disputes. International wars are often as disastrous to the victors as to the vanquished, and industrial wars are always so. The parties in this dispute must learn to rid themselves of that spirit of distrust and suspicion which only embitters strife and makes amicable relations impossible. Mutual good will can settle many things, but mutual antagonism can settle nothing. And as capital has an immense advantage in labor disputes because it controls the means of production, it can well afford to be magnanimous, to make the first advances, to offer to labor a more equitable share of the wealth which the latter helps to produce.

If a question should arise as to how this can best be done, I confess I see no better way at present than by the adoption, in most forms of productive industry, of the principle and practice of profit-sharing. This is no new thing. More than fifty years ago the experiment was tried in France by a single house, and so satisfactory were the results that the example set by Leclaire, of Paris, was followed in many other places; and before the end of 1880 upward of fifty industrial establishments in France, Alsace, and Switzerland alone were working on similar lines. Methods differ in different houses, especially in regard to details, but the underlying principle is the same, namely, that each permanent employee shall participate in a fixed part of the net profits of the business in proportion to what he receives as wages. I am unable to say to what extent the principle has been tried in England, but in the United States, three years ago, some ten thousand workmen were sharing the profits of the several industries in which they were engaged. In some cases, it must be confessed, the attempts were not successful; but the failures were due to unfavorable circumstances, or to lack of intelligent zeal in working out the system. All enterprises are not equally adapted to the process of profit-sharing, but experience has proved that the principle is capable of very wide application, and can be carried out to the mutual advantage of employers and employed. The best results are more easily attained in large establishments with a numerous staff, where participation in profits is only a nucleus for a wider circle of agencies having reference to the social, sanitary, educational, moral, and religious well-being of all the participants, and where the profit-sharing itself is upon a basis that promotes thrift, independence, self-respect, and prudent provision for the time of sickness or old age.

The advantages of such a system, wisely administered, are obvious and manifold. At the very outset it would go a long way toward removing that sense of injustice, whether well founded or not, which now embitters the feelings of so many workmen against their employers; it would place in a new light the relations of employer and employed, for the former would no longer be regarded a hard taskmaster, intent only on his own interests, and the latter would be something more than a bond servant, rendering unwilling service for a price that he considers below his value, but both would be partners in one great enterprise, where success means a real advantage to both, and where the highest success can be reached only through cordial coöperation. Such a system would reduce to a minimum losses caused by waste of time or material, or by defective workmanship; for every workman, being in a sense a partner in the concern, will quickly learn that to guard his own interests he must guard against loss of every kind; and this will lead to a perception of the further truth that his own interests and those of his employer are identical. Such a system would raise the character of the workmen, partly by imposing a new sense of responsibility, and partly by its tendency to weed out the indolent and the dishonest, and to relegate the inefficient to a lower grade of service, with poorer pay. The educational effect would be incalculable when it was found that it does not pay to employ inefficient workmen, even at lower wages, and that the way to well-paid work is open only to the skillful, the honest, and the efficient. Such a system would increase the productiveness of labor and improve the quality of what is produced, for it stands to reason that he who puts his heart into his task because he shares in the benefits will do more and better work than he who can look for no reward beyond his weekly wage. Above all, it will be a step, a long step, in the direction of improved social conditions for those by whom the world's work is done, and a prophecy of the coming time when all strife and contention shall cease because the causes of strife have been eliminated, and instead of mutual suspicion and antagonism between employer and employed there shall be mutual sympathy and confidence.

It would be very unwise to suppose that such a change in our industrial system can be brought about in a day. Selfishness, cupidity, and the jealousies resulting from embittered contests will be arrayed against it. Prophets of evil will predict disaster; business rivals will denounce a method which they are unwilling to adopt; while social agitators will antagonize a movement which, if successful, would reduce their influence to zero, and compel them to find some better employment. Worst of all, not a few of the very class who are most to be benefited will be hard to convince, and will attribute all kinds of sinister motives to the man who proposes so unusual a scheme as that of voluntarily sharing his profits with his workmen.[1] But patience and perseverance will overcome all these obstacles, and when at last the goal is won—when industrial peace takes the place of angry strife, and "good will toward men" becomes the ruling principle in business affairs—no Christian man will regret the sacrifice by which the results were accomplished, but with a thankful heart will exultingly exclaim, "The kingdom of heaven is at hand!"

---

[1] When Leclaire, of Paris, first proposed his method of profit-sharing, a section of his workmen, supported by a newspaper, assumed a hostile attitude, and he was accused of seeking to reduce wages. It was only by the first actual distribution of profits that he succeeded in convincing the workmen of the honesty of his intention.

LECTURE VI.

THE STABILITY, PERPETUITY, AND FINAL CONSUMMATION OF THE KINGDOM OF GOD.

"His kingdom is an everlasting kingdom, and his dominion is from generation to generation." (Dan. iv. 3.)

"The kingdom of the world is become the kingdom of our Lord, and of his Christ: and he shall reign forever and ever." (Rev. xi. 15.)

"My purpose is . . . to indicate a little more definitely what the results of such an obedience as I have proposed will be in what we are accustomed to think of as the distinctly Christian field—that is, what will ensue when men who call themselves Christians begin seriously to accept and really to obey the plain commandments of the historical personage, Jesus of Nazareth; commandments which, hitherto, we have been satisfied to quote with appropriately pious unction, and dismiss with religious alacrity." (Rev. William Bayard Hale, "The New Obedience," p. 19.)

"My hope for the future is in the ideal of Christ. My hope for man is a more perfect and complete embodiment of the Christian religion. When I look abroad and see the disintegrative agencies that are hard at work, the one thing I am anxious to do is to bring the great constructive . . . principles of our Christian faith into relation with life and action. Every Christian principle embodied in law or society, every Christian deed accomplished in industry, helps on the happier time." (Principal Fairbairn, "Religion in History and in Modern Life," p. 260.)

VI.

*PRELUDE.—SOCIALISM THE WORLD'S COUNTER-
FEIT OF THE KINGDOM OF GOD.*

AN old Puritan divine is credited with the remark that "whenever the Almighty sets up his Church in a place, the devil is sure to set up his chapel beside it." In other words, evil does its work by counterfeiting something that is good rather than by showing itself in its own colors. Paul, describing this process, tells how " Satan fashioneth himself into an angel of light," and warns us to expect that his ministers may do the same. Thus bigotry and intolerance masquerade in the garments of religious zeal; uncharitableness and evil speaking are defended as fidelity to truth; the partisan wears the mask of the patriot while exploiting his country for his own advantage; false Christs go forth into the world claiming the homage which belongs to the true Christ; science offers itself as a substitute for revelation, and reason usurps the place of faith; instead of "the city which hath the foundations," we are pointed to airy places in the cloudland of some social Utopia, and the advent of democratic socialism is heralded as the world's real millennium, instead of the reign of the kingdom of God.

But before conceding so large a claim it may be well to ascertain, if we can, just what socialism is, what it proposes to do, and by what means it expects to accomplish its purpose. This is by no means an easy task. The question, What is socialism? is one which vast numbers who call themselves socialists cannot answer, and of which many of its advocates have only a vague and confused notion. The fact is, there is socialism and socialism, and the word does not always mean the same thing. Used in its widest sense, the word might include almost every social movement of which history gives us any account, from the mildest form of voluntary communism to the most radical form of compulsory State socialism. But in this discussion we must define the term more carefully, and restrict its meaning within much narrower limits. Professor Janet touches the root of the matter when he says: "We call socialism every doctrine which teaches that the State has a right to correct the inequality of wealth which exists among men, and to legally establish the balance by taking from those who have too much in order to give to those who have not enough, and that in a permanent manner, and not in such and such a particular case—a famine, for instance, a public calamity, etc." [1]

Laveleye expresses himself on similar lines. "In the first place," he remarks, "every socialistic doctrine aims at introducing greater equality in social conditions; and in the second place, at realizing those reforms by the law of the State." [1] What we have in mind is the socialism that has made such headway on the continent of Europe, especially in Germany, the most distinguished advocate and representative of which is the late Karl Marx.

Socialism of the type just referred to aims at a complete transformation of the present industrial system. Private capital is to be replaced by collective capital, and there is to be common ownership of all the means of production. This would abolish at a stroke the present competitive system. Private business and enterprise would cease. All productive labor would be equipped out of collective capital, on the basis of the collective ownership of all working materials of labor, and both production and distribution would be controlled and directed by persons in the receipt of salaries. All private profits would cease, and wages, as at

---

[1] Quoted by T Kirkup in Introduction to "A History of Socialism."

present understood, would no longer be paid, but each workman would receive a share of the products in proportion to the social value of his labor. This principle would extend to those who are not producers, but who render useful service of other kinds to the community, such as judges, doctors, public officials, teachers, scientific investigators, and the like. These statements supply only a meager outline of the vast revolutionary scheme of modern socialism, but they suffice to show that for its realization society will require an organization as complete and a discipline as absolute as that of an army in the field; and unless the system is to degenerate into an utter despotism, and labor be exploited worse than before, this industrial army must be officered through all its camps by men of not only transcendent ability, but of absolutely incorruptible integrity, with an unselfishness of aim and a readiness of self-sacrifice never yet witnessed save in Jesus the Christ and in those men and women who have followed closely in his footsteps.

It is a well-known fact that in society, as at present constituted, the chief difficulty is to find men of sufficient capacity to organize and direct vast industrial movements; of sufficient integrity to be intrusted with large financial interests; of such undoubted ability and such lofty patriotism that to them can be committed, without fear, the gravest affairs of State. Industrial and financial corporations are eagerly looking for such men, and when one is found they are willing to pay a very large price to secure his services; while in public affairs any nation that found itself in possession of a group of men of exceptional sagacity and incorruptible integrity to whom it might safely intrust its destinies would consider itself happy and favored beyond all other nations in the world. Now socialism, as I understand it, expects to accomplish all this, on an infinitely larger scale, while systematically repressing the chief incentives to the highest endeavor by abolishing the rewards which, under the present industrial system, are the sure harvest of success. It expects to find men who can organize and direct schemes so vast and complicated that the most gigantic enterprises of the present system are dwarfed by comparison; who can exercise autocratic power without abusing it; and who can have unlimited opportunities for peculation without falling into the snare. And these men of transcendent ability, of impartial justice, of unimpeachable honesty, must be found in the ranks of the present captains of industry whom socialistic agitators are never weary of denouncing as tyrants and robbers of the worst type.

Considering the diverse views of many socialistic writers, and the vague notions entertained by others, it is quite likely that some will take exception to my statements as an unfair representation of the principles and aims of socialism. The fact is that thus far the leaders of socialism have been very reticent, as Dr. Schäffle observes, in announcing a definite or positive programme.[1] As a rule they content themselves, and very wisely so, with assailing the present industrial and social systems, which are fairly open to attack in many directions. Unlike Christianity, socialism has no "sacred books" to which inquisitive critics might be referred as containing an authoritative statement of its principles; and we can only infer from the writings of recognized leaders what the new system will be and do. Still, those who are familiar with the theories propounded by leading thinkers in the socialistic ranks will not regard my statements as overdrawn.

But how does socialism propose ultimately to bring about this great industrial revolution? The answer is plain: By a system of wholesale confiscation; or, to use the euphemistic term of the

---

[1] The student of socialistic literature will readily recognize the author's indebtedness to Dr. Schäffle in some parts of this prelude.

socialists, by "expropriation." Under the new *régime*, "society," or the "State," is to take possession—peaceably if it can, forcibly if it must—of all the means and materials of production, such as land, buildings, manufactories, tools, machinery, raw materials, and the like; not necessarily without compensation, but the compensation, if any, would be in the form of barter—in food supplies, clothing, furniture, or even articles of luxury, but nothing that could be converted into capital, or used as such. This, at least, is what the more liberal-minded socialists propose; but whether it will or can be carried out when socialism comes to its own, is quite another question. Marx undertakes to show how the capitalistic system grew out of the destruction of small ownerships, in which the workman was owner of his tools and of the produce of his work. When this has been largely accomplished then the great capitalist attacks the smaller, creating vast monopolies, the result of which is affirmed to be " a growing mass of misery, oppression, slavery, degradation, exploitation." But along with this there is springing up an organization of labor and a revolt of the working class against existing conditions, and when this has reached a certain stage then " the knell of capitalist property sounds. The expropriators are the expropriated." "In the former case," he adds, "we had the expropriation of the masses of the people by a few usurpers; in the latter we have the expropriation of a few usurpers by the masses of the people."[1] The morality of all this seems to be that when the many take property from the few without their consent, and possibly without compensation, it is a virtue; but when the few obtain property from the many, even by fair exchange, it is a crime. In other words, the accumulation of individuals, no matter how obtained, is criminal, but the forcible expropriation of such wealth by the State is not. Lawrence Gronlund, a socialist of the Marx school, puts the case in its baldest form thus: "Every millionaire is a criminal. Every one who amasses a hundred thousand dollars is a criminal. Every one who loans his neighbor one hundred dollars, and exacts one hundred and six in return, is a criminal."[2]

This is sufficiently plain; and the same writer, "in the course of a conjectural discussion of the ways in which socialism may be realized," does not seem to object altogether to dynamite as a last resort.[3]

---

[1] Karl Marx, "Das Kapital," concluding chapter.
[2] Quoted by Dr. Gladden, "Applied Christianity," p. 83.
[3] *Ibid.*, p. 74.

But what place are Christianity and Christian ethics to occupy in the socialistic scheme of the future? As far as I can understand it, they will have no place at all, if the more pronounced socialists can have their way. Undoubtedly Dr. Schäffle is right in saying that " socialism of the present day is out and out irreligious, and hostile to the Church. It says that the Church is only a police institution for upholding capital, and that it deceives the common people with a ' check payable in heaven'; that the Church deserves to perish." [1]

If this be so, we may safely conclude that when socialism sweeps away private capital it will sweep away, if it can, what it seems to regard as the chief buttress of private capital. Nor will the ethics of Christianity fare much better if Mr. Gronlund, whom I have already quoted, may be taken as a representative of socialistic views. "Children," he tells us, "do not belong to their parents; they belong to society." And again: " In the very nature of things family supremacy will be absolutely incompatible with an *interdependent*, solidaric commonwealth, for in such a state the first object of education must be to establish in the minds of the children an indissoluble association between

---

[1] "Quintessence of Socialism," Humboldt Library ed., p. 85.

their individual happiness and the good of all. To that end family exclusiveness must be broken down first of all." [1] Now whatever be the political unit of the nation, the family is the social unit, and whatever assails the sacredness and integrity of the home is antichristian—an undisguised foe of society as well as of the kingdom of God.

While socialism and the kingdom of God rest upon widely different foundations, and pursue their ends by different means, the results aimed at are, to some extent at least, the same—namely, an era of universal brotherhood, the improvement of social conditions, the reign of social justice and good will; in a word, they both aim—professedly at least—at bringing about an ideal condition of society, in which oppression and injustice, and the poverty which causes suffering, shall cease to be. But Christianity proposes something which finds no place in the programme of socialism, but which is an essential factor in securing the results aimed at, namely, the regeneration of the individual. Socialism seeks certain results of Christianity, but repudiates its process. It seeks the temporal benefits of Christianity, but spurns its ethical teaching and will not submit to its discipline. It demands

---

[1] Quoted by Dr. Gladden, "Applied Christianity," p. 85.

social justice, but repudiates moral righteousness. It claims unlimited rights, but seems to recognize no corresponding obligations. It proceeds upon the principle of "what is yours is mine, and what is mine is my own." Try to disguise it as they may, the foundation of political socialism is selfishness.

There are three great social agencies at work in the world to-day—namely, anarchism, socialism, and Christianity. Anarchism is uncontrolled individualism running amuck through society, its spirit destructive, its outcome savagery. Secular socialism is democracy lashing itself into fury; Demos without a master, liable, when a favorable moment comes, to repeat the history to which Tennyson refers, when "Celtic Demos rose a demon, shrieked, and slaked the light with blood."[1] Christianity is society organizing itself on a basis of righteousness and good will, the friend of all, the enemy of none. Anarchism proposes to *abolish* society by violence, and to introduce a social chaos wherein every man shall do only what is right in his own eyes. Socialism proposes to *reconstruct* society by a wholesale expropriation, and to introduce a system which must inevitably end in social

---

[1] "Sixty Years After," st. 45.

despotism. Christianity proposes to *regenerate* society by a mighty spiritual force, and to introduce the era of universal brotherhood by a radical change in man himself, and not merely in his environment. Anarchists of the pronounced type are not mistaken men to be reasoned with, nor ordinary criminals to be restrained; they are dangerous madmen whom society should not suffer to be at large. Socialists of the pronounced type are, for the most part, mischievous agitators, stirring up selfish passions which they cannot allay, and leading the mob they know not whither, in chase of shadows that can never be grasped. Christians, no matter how pronounced, may sometimes be unwise, and even the best of them may come short of their own ideal, but while they are true to the laws of the kingdom of God they can work no ill to society, but only good.

When I speak of socialism as the world's counterfeit of the kingdom of God, I mean chiefly that form of socialism which is secular, materialistic, and, in its logical outcome, atheistic. This is the socialism with which Christianity will have to reckon in the near future. It dominates the movement in Europe, and to a large extent in America. I am well aware that there are men who are called— or who call themselves—socialists, but who have taken the disease in a mild form, who would repudiate, on their own behalf at least, the statement just made; but careful observers of modern tendencies know that what I say is true. That there is a measure of truth underlying the arguments of democratic socialism I do not deny. If it were all false, it could do nothing, for unmixed falsehood can make no permanent headway. It is because of the truth that is in it that socialism is able to counterfeit the kingdom of God. But, as Joseph Cook said of spiritism, the truth is like a jewel in a toad's head: the jewel is very small, and the toad is very large and very slimy.

While socialism announces some objects which are in line with Christian teaching, its methods, for the most part, are antichristian. Anarchism teaches that society is nothing and the individual is everything; socialism teaches that the individual is nothing and society is everything; Christ teaches that both are of infinite value, but that the highest good of society can be secured only by regenerating and saving the individual, so that in turn he may contribute to the regeneration of society. Socialism proposes to take forcible possession of all the means of production, and to divide the products on the basis of labor; Christ proposes to take possession of nothing, save the human heart, and to divide nothing; but lays down the principle that each man's possessions are a personal trust to be administered as conscience and Providence may direct. Socialism, by its doctrine of state paternalism, subverts the principle of self-help, and leads men to depend upon others rather than upon their own exertions; Christ teaches his followers to labor with all diligence so that they may have to give to him that needeth.[1] Socialism prohibits freedom of acquisition by removing its chief incentive; Christ places no arbitrary limit, provided all accumulations be held as a trust and so administered. Socialism would remove inequalities of condition by the hatred of the poor against the rich; Christ would correct them by teaching the rich to love and help the poor.

In points like these and a hundred more the difference between the two systems appears, and should convince every thoughtful Christian that secular socialism is the irreconcilable foe of the kingdom of God. How dangerous this foe may become only time can tell, but I sometimes think that perhaps prophecy may yet receive its most startling fulfillment along this line. Listen to this from the second chapter of Second Thessalonians:

---

[1] Acts xx. 35; Ephesians iv. 28.

"Now we beseech you, brethren, touching the coming of our Lord Jesus Christ, and our gathering together unto him; to the end that ye be not quickly shaken from your mind, nor yet be troubled, either by spirit, or by word, or by epistle as from us, as that the day of the Lord is *now* present; let no man beguile you in anywise, for *it will not be*, except the falling away come first, and the man of sin be revealed, the son of perdition, he that opposeth and exalteth himself against all that is called God or that is worshiped, so that he sitteth in the temple of God, setting himself forth as God. . . . For the mystery of lawlessness doth already work: only there is one that restraineth now, until he be taken out of the way. And then shall be revealed the lawless one, whom the Lord Jesus shall slay with the breath of his mouth, and bring to naught by the manifestation of his coming; *even he*, whose coming is according to the working of Satan with all signs and lying wonders, and with all deceit of unrighteousness for them that are perishing; because they received not the love of the truth, that they might be saved."

Whether this will receive its full accomplishment in the logical developments of atheistic socialism the future must reveal. Meanwhile, "he that hath ears to hear, let him hear."

LECTURE VI.—THE STABILITY, PERPETUITY, AND FINAL CONSUMMATION OF THE KINGDOM OF GOD.

THE history of astronomical discovery presents some of the most wonderful triumphs of the human intellect to be found in the whole range of scientific investigations. The problems encountered were so intricate, the conditions so complex, the objects to be examined so distant, their movements so shrouded, their reciprocal influence so mysterious, that one could not wonder if the task had been abandoned in despair. But a healthy human mind is so constituted that difficulties only brace it for more resolute effort, and a course of investigation once begun is continued with a tenacity of purpose that knows not the meaning of defeat, but is pursued century after century, if need be, till victory crown its endeavors. In early ages the investigator had to make his way, slowly and laboriously, through a labyrinth of isolated and seemingly conflicting phenomena, without the aid of those appliances which now render observation comparatively easy; but when at length his patience and devotion were rewarded by the discovery of the great laws of motion and universal gravitation, astronomy was at once elevated to the dignity of a science, and the pathway for future investigators was made plain.

But the path, though plain, was by no means easy. While each step of progress marked the passage of barriers that once seemed to be insurmountable, new problems of still greater complexity were constantly arising, and difficulties increased in almost geometrical ratio. But former triumphs stimulated to fresh endeavor, and the human mind rose to meet each new emergency with an undaunted courage that gave assurance of success. When observing the motions of a sun and a single planet, or of a planet and its satellite, the problems awaiting solution were comparatively simple; but with the discovery of each additional planet, satellite, or even asteroid, the complexity of the problem was greatly increased. For it had already been demonstrated that these bodies were not isolated orbs, but a family of worlds, each reciprocally influencing every other. Throughout the whole system " planet sways planet, and satellite bends the orbit of satellite, until the primitive curves lose the simplicity of their character, and perturbations arise which may end in absolute destruction." [1]

---

[1] Professor Mitchell.

The great problem involved the question of the stability of the entire planetary system, and its solution required a delicacy of observation and a power of mathematical analysis that approached the superhuman. It is not necessary to follow in detail the lines of investigation, and I need do little more than state results. Suffice it to say that in the movements of the planets and their satellites several distinct forces are at work. First, there is the primitive impulse by which they were projected through space, and in obedience to which, if free from any disturbing influence, they would have moved in a straight line forever. Secondly, the central power lodged in the sun, by which the planets are drawn into circular or elliptical orbits. Thirdly, the mutual influence of the planets upon each other. A knowledge of these forces gave rise to two important questions, the first of which was: Will the central power by which the sun draws a planet to itself finally overcome the original impulse, so that the orbit will diminish till at the last the planet will plunge bodily into the sun? Rigorous mathematical analysis has answered the question by showing that the amount by which the central power overcomes in a moment of time the effect of the primitive impulse is so infinitesimally small that it would become appreciable only at the end of a period infinitely long, repeated an infinite number of times.

The second question was: Will the mutual attraction of the planets on each other so change the form of their orbits as to result in the destruction of the system? Observation had shown that the forms of the planetary orbits were really changing; and if these changes should prove to be progressive in one direction, without compensation, the destruction of the system was inevitable. Here again it is impossible to even catalogue the facts involved in this intricate investigation, or to explain the methods of its solution. Suffice it to say that unsparing analysis has demonstrated that the changes in the form of the planetary orbits are not permanently progressive in one direction, but within certain periods of vast duration are entirely compensated, so that the orbits return to their primitive values. Changes there are, but they are within ascertained limits, and so, vibrating to and fro in periods which stun the imagination, the limits are assigned beyond which the changes can never pass. Millions of years will elapse before these marvelous movements will have run their course, and the whole system return to the exact condition in which it was when the primitive impulse was given; but the result is sure; the system is stable. It does not, so far as motion is concerned, carry within it the seeds of its own destruction, and we may rest assured that He who planned this wonderful system does not intend that it shall wear out or fall to pieces before a single revolution of its complicated machinery has been accomplished, and the great bell of eternity has sounded—ONE!

Turning from the physical to the moral and spiritual spheres, we are confronted by a similar problem. There are movements in the realms of mind and morals as well as in the realm of matter. Influences are at work which give rise to serious perturbations in courses of human action which, if continuous without compensation in one direction, would seem to threaten the overthrow of religion and of the morality which is based upon it. Stated in other words, the problem is this: Is the kingdom of God stable? Can it so withstand the strain of antagonistic forces, without or within, that its permanence may be regarded as assured? If not, it must be because it holds within itself, like the kingdoms of this world, the seeds of decay and ultimate destruction, or else that the external forces arrayed against it are too strong to be overcome.

In the investigations of modern science new expressions have come into use to represent new ideas. One of these is the "conservation of energy," or the doctrine that the sum total of the energy of the universe neither diminishes nor increases, although it may assume in succession a diversity of forms; another is the "persistence of force," which is based upon the supposed indestructibility of matter and energy. Assuming that these expressions convey corresponding truths, it is clear that they cannot be limited in their application to the material universe alone. Energy belongs to the spiritual realm as truly as it does to the physical, although the energy is of a different kind and is exerted for a different purpose; and force is quite as persistent in the former realm as in the latter. In the nature of things it must be so; for while physical energy is due, as far as we know, to the action and interaction of purely physical causes, spiritual energy has its source in a divine life, implanted and sustained by the Spirit of God; and this life has in it no seeds of destruction or decay. It may be forfeited by an individual, or be withdrawn from a disobedient Church, but cannot in itself decline or become corrupt; and as this divine life is of the very essence of the kingdom of God among men, the future of that kingdom, as regards stability, cannot be in any degree uncertain.

This view finds striking confirmation in the pages of history. Look for a moment at the condition of affairs when the kingdom of God first entered the lists to measure strength with the kingdoms of this world. The Founder of the divine kingdom had recently been put to death as a malefactor, and his very name was a byword and a reproach. His followers were very few in number, and entirely destitute of that influence which comes from wealth or high social standing. To the Jew their gospel was a "stumbling-block," to the Greek it was "foolishness," and yet it was "by the foolishness of preaching" the gospel that they proposed to conquer the world. Could anything be more Utopian? And, as if to crown the apparent absurdity, this task was not undertaken at a time when the human intellect had become enfeebled, when systems of government had become effete, when jurisprudence and statesmanship had exhausted their resources in a vain attempt to establish justice and judgment in the earth. On the contrary, it was just when the wisdom of the world's most astute philosophers, the military skill of its greatest generals, the splendor of its unrivaled art, the statecraft of its mightiest kings, had culminated in the magnificent empire of the Cæsars, and when the human mind seemed best fitted to grapple with the problems of society and government.

That such a time should be chosen for the definite advent of a heavenly kingdom seems strange to the last degree. And when we consider that the new kingdom was to be based upon principles that had never before been tried in the affairs of government; that it was to be the exponent of principles that must inevitably bring it into collision with the established kingdoms of the world; that force was to be utterly excluded from its methods of extension and government, and never employed even in self-defense; that, so far from seeking to revenge injuries, it would never retaliate, save by returning good for evil; that it placed itself in direct antagonism to the very things which the world regarded as indispensable; that it did not conceal its purpose of revolutionizing human governments, of combating the world's philosophers, of overturning hoary systems intrenched behind the superstitions of ages, until the whole face of society would be changed; we may surely conclude that he who could propose such an undertaking, at such a time, must have been dominated by the wildest enthusiasm, or else upheld by the serene consciousness of power divine.

Judged by ordinary human standards, the whole scheme was visionary in the highest degree. To all appearance Christianity was the feeblest and most obscure force operating in society. Against it were arrayed the contempt of the learned and wise, the arrogance of wealth, the cruelty of superstition, the intolerance of religious bigotry, backed by the power of the mightiest empire the world had ever known, resolute in its purpose to exterminate a sect that was everywhere spoken against, and to overthrow utterly a kingdom that had the audacity to avow that it owed no allegiance to the kingdom of this world. But notwithstanding the tremendous odds arrayed against it, the growth of the new kingdom became the marvel of history. It overcame the prejudice of the Jew, changed the wisdom of the Greek into foolishness, softened the stern heart of the Roman, overturned the altars of heathenism, established a new code of ethics, brought a fresh lease of life to a dying world, and turned the currents of history into channels entirely new. By the power of that faith which was its animating principle the kingdom of God, even in its infancy, "subdued kingdoms, wrought righteousness, obtained promises, stopped the mouths of lions, quenched the power of fire, escaped the edge of the sword, from weakness were made strong, waxed mighty in war, turned to flight armies of aliens." And this marvelous "persistence of force" is a guarantee of the stability and perpetuity of the kingdom for all time to come.

But suppose the facts to be substantially as I have stated them, does that really guarantee the future of the kingdom? It is true that Christianity won marvelous triumphs in a ruder age, and more than held its own in the face of such forces as could then be arrayed against it; but can it do the same thing now? Times have greatly changed, and men have changed with them. If ignorance was once the mother of devotion, as some one has affirmed, may not intelligence become its most dangerous foe? Christianity withstood the arrows of the ancient barbarian; can it withstand the polished shafts of the modern skeptic? It feared not to encounter the speculative wisdom of the Greek; but how about the science of the Anglo-Saxon? Its miracles passed muster in an age of superstition; but how will it be now when the searchlights of science, turned to every quarter of the universe, have failed to find the supernatural? Once it could fall back upon an assumption of authority, when a "thus saith the Lord" was deemed a sufficient answer to every objection; but how about to-day when all authority is challenged, and even the genuineness of the sacred books is called in question?

To all this it may be answered, in general terms, that there is no reason to anticipate in the future more bitter or more dangerous attacks upon Christianity than it has sustained in the past; and if former assaults have failed to shake its foundations, there is no reason to think that future assaults will be more successful. There is scarcely one department of science or system of philosophy which has not at some time or other been pressed into service against the truth and kingdom of God. Biology in its infancy sneered at the idea that God was the sole Author and Giver of life, and the doctrine of spontaneous generation was boastingly proclaimed; but time and experiment revealed the mistakes of the methods and the absurdity of the conclusions, and to-day there is no biologist of repute who does not accept and teach the doctrine that life can come only from antecedent life. Professor Tyndall is an unprejudiced witness, and he says: "I affirm that no shred of trustworthy experimental testimony exists to prove that life in our day has ever appeared independently of antecedent life."[1]

Astronomy thought that it had discovered glaring mistakes, not only in the Mosaic cosmogomy but in the actual structure of the universe, and that it would be easy to plan creation in more perfect accord with the eternal and immutable laws of math-

---

[1] *Nineteenth Century*, 1878, p. 507.

ematics; but in time it became clear that the Author of the universe was not only an almighty Creator, but also an infinite Geometer, who in the completion of his creative work had produced not a chaos but a cosmos, every part established, balanced, adjusted, with a mathematical precision that man in his best works but feebly and distantly imitates.

Archæology, too, has muttered with antiquated voice against the antiquity of the sacred records, and from the buried past monuments have been unearthed which at one time were thought to prove that Moses was mistaken, and the Bible unworthy of credence; but to-day the uncovered ruins of Babylon and Nineveh, with their indelible records of a remote antiquity, come forth to testify, and while men in whom the wish is father to the thought are affirming that the Mosaic records are disproved, lo! "the stone" cries "out of the wall, and the beam out of the timber" answers it, saying: "The word of our God shall stand forever." Last of all, Geology, youngest of the physical sciences, must needs try its hand, and there are men still living who remember how some of its early discoveries, so called, were hailed as unanswerable evidences of the mistakes of Moses. Two favorite points of attack were the six creative days and the story of the flood. But it is well to note that the biblical record of these two events can be made to do service against Christian belief only by interpreting the record in a most crude and literal way, and, in regard to one of them at least, by rejecting the latest discoveries of geological science. Regarding the deluge it may be said that its occurrence and general character are made probable by a remarkable consensus in the traditions of all ancient nations, confirmed by the engraved tablets recently unearthed at Babylon, and further confirmed by the discoveries of Quaternary geology. These discoveries have proved beyond dispute that during the latest geologic period, and since man came upon the stage, there has been a deep submergence of immense land areas, far below the surface of the waters, with corresponding elevations of perhaps equal areas, whereby beds of marine shells once on the sea bottom were lifted, and are now found on mountain sides or summits hundreds of feet above the present ocean level. If these discoveries have not sufficed to convince scientists with skeptical tendencies that the Bible account is scientifically true, they have at least taught most of them not to be too hasty in their generalizations, and not to jump at conclusions before the necessary data are at hand.

What, then, on the whole, is the outlook for the stability of the kingdom of God—the permanence of the Church and her institutions? We live in times when, as Joseph Cook puts it, everything is shaken that can be shaken, and everything that can be shaken ought to be shaken. In the mighty shaking that is going on, the shaking of creed and system and dogmatic statement, and even daring attempts to shake the word of God itself, there would seem to be a fulfillment, in another sense than the more obvious one, of that word: "Yet once more I shake not the earth only, but also heaven. And this word, Yet once more, signifieth the removing of those things that are shaken, as of things that are made, that those things which cannot be shaken may remain."[1] So let it be. Whatsoever can be shaken let it be shaken, and the sooner the better. We do not want to be found amid rotten foundations and crumbling pillars and crashing roof in the day when the earthquake shock shall try every man's work of what sort it is. But in the future, as in the past, "the things which cannot be shaken" will "remain." Many a rash hand has been laid upon the pillars of eternal truth—upon miracle and

---

[1] Hebrews xii. 26, 27.

prophecy, incarnation and atonement—as though they were only supports for the roof of some Dagon temple of effete superstition; but, founded upon the Rock of Ages, the mighty columns stand unshaken still. And when all that man has built upon other foundations shall have left only a ruin to tell where once the structure stood, the eternal purpose of God shall stand, "a kingdom which cannot be moved."

But what about the consummation of the kingdom? Clearly it has not yet reached the limits of its development. Those ideal conditions foreshadowed in the Christian millennium are still in the future, and some do not hesitate to affirm that we are, if possible, farther from their realization than ever before. I cannot indorse such a pessimistic view. Social as well as civil and religious conditions show vast improvement, and the race has advanced a long distance millenniumward in even the last two hundred years. Those who deny this are simply ignorant of the history of the past and the facts of the present. Who would be willing, if he had the power, to turn back the shadow on the dial of the world's progress by even two hundred years, and land us in those times when, in what was misnamed "good" society, manners and morals were coarse beyond description, when conversation, to be appreciated, must be liberally seasoned with profanity; when after-dinner talk was of such a character that ladies must leave the room before it began, and when it was considered no disgrace for gentlemen to fall under the table in a state of helpless intoxication? Shall we go back to the time when women convicted of offenses were publicly whipped, when prisoners were set in the pillory to be pelted and jeered by the mob, and when the branding of criminals and the cropping of their ears was a common practice? Were those times better than these, when to be poor or insane was worse than death itself; when almshouses and asylums were almost unknown, and the maintenance of the poor was sold by auction to the lowest bidder, who was left to treat the helpless wretches very much as he pleased? Shall we revert to the time, say two hundred years ago, when popular education, in any sense worthy of the term, had not made a beginning, and when men like Governor Berkeley, of Virginia, could say, " I thank God that we have no free schools or printing presses; . . . God keep us from both"?[1] Shall we heave one sigh of regret for those " good old times " of which we sometimes hear, when, in

---

[1] Quoted by Minot J. Savage, D.D., in *Arena*, December, 1890, p. 15.

the material sphere, railways and steamships, telegraphs and telephones, gas and electricity, were yet undreamed of; when in the industrial sphere the ordinary workman was no better than a slave, forbidden by law to assemble in public meetings or form any organization to promote his own interests, and when the skilled artisan received less wages and was no better housed or fed than the poorest skilled laborer of to-day; when in the domestic sphere no provision was made for the education of women, and there was no higher conception of woman's mission than to be the slave of man's passions or the drudge of his home; when in the moral sphere there were no abstinence societies to check the spread of intemperance, or healthy sentiment to repress public immorality or social vice; when in the social sphere there were no associations for the alleviation of poverty and suffering, or the improvement of social conditions; and when in the religious sphere there were no convictions of duty respecting the world's evangelization, but a prevalent spirit of religious indifference on the one hand, and on the other of bigotry and intolerance that was more concerned about internal disputes than outward aggression, and attached more importance to dogma and Church order than to charity of spirit and righteousness of life?

No, no. The "former times" were not "better than these." The kingdom of God has been going forward, not backward. It faces the sunrise, and the time draws near when its "sun shall no more go down." The moral tone of society is higher, and the common conscience is far more sensitive, than ever before. Appeals for aid in religious and benevolent work meet a readier and more generous response, both in the way of gifts and personal service. No small share of the brain and heart of the world is now enlisted in whatever makes for the uplifting of mankind. Human brotherhood is no longer the dream of an enthusiast, but the sober belief of thoughtful men, and social justice, once regarded as an unattainable Utopia, is brought within measurable distance in the purpose and plan of the kingdom of God.

What, then, is wanted to usher in that consummation of the heavenly kingdom which prophets foresaw and of which the world still idly dreams? Will it be accomplished by some new spiritual force, as yet unheard of, which God in his own good time will bring to bear upon society, revolutionizing present conditions by a power that cannot be resisted? I see no reason to expect such an intervention, for we have no hint in nature or in revelation of any new moral or spiritual power outside of those already known to men. It is true that many are asking in these days concerning the Christ, as did the disciples whom John sent: "Art thou he that should come, or do we look for another?"[1] And some tell us that they are listening with the poet for the bells that will "ring in the Christ that is to be," as though the Christ of Bethlehem and Calvary were a myth, and his very name a worn-out spell. But, believe me, the Christ that is now is the Christ that is to be, and there is no other. If the question of the regeneration of society were solely a question of divine power, we might well wonder why that power has slumbered so long; but if it is a question of moral forces, in which man's consent and voluntary self-surrender are indispensable factors, it may turn out that what the world is waiting for is already within its reach.

The world needs no new gospel, but only an unfeigned acceptance of a gospel already proclaimed. "Talk about the questions of the day," said Gladstone; "there is but one question, and that is the gospel. It can and will correct everything needing correction." Most true, but only in so far as that gospel is accepted and obeyed. Not by the

---

[1] Matthew xi. 3.

"enthusiasm of humanity" can this sinning, suffering world be uplifted, and the kingdom of God be established among men. Neither will it be by the enthusiasm of dogma, which has often made void the word of God by its traditions; nor by the enthusiasm of denominational zeal, more concerned about the accent of its shibboleth than about "judgment, mercy, and the love of God"; nor by the enthusiasm of the political demagogue, inflaming the passions that need to be allayed, and deluding the mutitude for selfish ends; nor by the enthusiasm of social theorists, who think to cleanse the sepulcher of society by an external coat of whitewash, and to abolish poverty and the suffering which comes of it by taking taxes from one pocket instead of two. Not by such forms of enthusiasm as these will the kingdom of the world be overthrown and the kingdom of God be set up in its place, but by the enthusiasm of *obedience*, when Christ's followers shall have learned that his words are not mere rhetorical flourishes to be admired, or *dogmata* about which to dispute; but plain, unmistakable precepts to be accepted and obeyed.

Let us now consider for a moment what the results would be if the laws of the kingdom of God were accepted as the rule of life in all our social relations—that is, if men would allow the golden rule to dominate their conduct in everything relating to their fellow-men. Beyond question, the first and most marked results would be in the kingdom itself. Those things which have been a standing reproach to Christianity and have hindered its progress would be at once and forever removed. Strife and discord would cease, and the causes which have rent and divided the Church of God would be seen in their true littleness and insignificance. Among the denominations coöperation would take the place of competition, and each would be anxious to help instead of hindering the others, waiting for the better day when they all shall be one. Brother would no longer go to law with brother, having in remembrance the words of the Lord Jesus: "If ye forgive men their trespasses, your heavenly Father will also forgive you."[1] The law of a real brotherhood would obliterate class distinctions, and oneness in Christ would be something more than a form of words. Property, no longer regarded as a private possession, but as a sacred trust to be administered for the common good, would cease to be the supreme object of desire. Poverty that would in any sense involve suffering would not exist, for there would

---

[1] Matthew vi. 14, 15.

be enough for all, and "distributing to the necessity of saints" would no longer be an irksome task, but a source of perennial joy. Greed and covetousness would cease to be factors in shaping human conduct, for when private rights are surrendered the most powerful motive prompting men to accumulate vast wealth would no longer operate. Best of all, with a return of primitive obedience would come a return of primitive blessing; and the Holy Spirit, no longer grieved and banished by man's disobedience, would return and dwell among his people, guiding their councils, directing their service, vitalizing all their works with divine life and power.

But not alone within the limits of the kingdom would results like these be seen, but universal society would feel the leavening power of a living Christianity, and its methods and maxims, its laws and customs, would show a corresponding change. Even in its present condition of imperfect development the kingdom of God has influenced the course of human history and modified the policy of nations to a vastly greater extent than is commonly supposed. Only let there be a return to first principles, and there will be a return of the ancient power. As a city set on a hill the kingdom of God will not be hid; as the salt of the earth it will save universal society from corruption and decay; as a leaven it will permeate human thought and human plans and institutions until the whole mass is leavened. And then shall dawn the day for which the world so long has waited, when the reign of universal brotherhood shall usher in the reign of universal peace; when men will have learned that not in strife and antagonism, but in mutual helpfulness and good will, lies the solution of our social problems, and that helpfulness and good will invariably spring from the same source—the love of God shed abroad in the heart. To some that day may seem far distant, for they think the obstacles in the way are too great to be overcome; but that is because they have never seen the full power which a living Christianity can wield when its precepts are accepted as a rule of life and its votaries live out the religion they profess. I do not mean to teach that the religion of Jesus, when thus lived, will at once win the admiration and love of men. On the contrary, they will despise it, hate it, crucify it if they can; but though they bury it never so deep, " on the third day " it " will rise again," radiant in heavenly beauty, triumphant after seeming defeat; overcoming greed and selfishness by the might of an invincible patience, conquering human pride and hatred by the power of omnipotent love.

www.ingramcontent.com/pod-product-compliance
Lightning Source LLC
Chambersburg PA
CBHW021353230426
43666CB00006B/516